Fodor's®99
Pocket
Phoenix &
Scottsdale

Excerpted from *Fodor's Arizona '99*

Fodor's Travel Publications, Inc.
New York • Toronto • London • Sydney • Auckland
www.fodors.com

Pocket Phoenix & Scottsdale

EDITORS: David Downing, Christina Knight

Editorial Contributors: David Brown, Daniel Mangin, Rich Rubin, Helayne Schiff, M. T. Schwartzman (Essential Information editor), Howard Seftel, Kim Westerman

Editorial Production: Nicole Revere

Maps: David Lindroth, Inc.; Mapping Specialists, *cartographer*; Steven K. Amsterdam, *map editor*

Design: Fabrizio La Rocca, *creative director*; Guido Caroti, *associate art director*; Lyndell Brookhouse-Gil, *cover designer*; Jolie Novak, *photo editor*

Production/Manufacturing: Mike Costa

Cover Photograph: Randy Prentice

Copyright

Special Sales

Fodor's Travel Publications are available at special discounts for bulk purchases for sales promotions or premiums. Special editions, including personalized covers, excerpts of existing guides, and corporate imprints, can be created in large quantities for special needs. For more information, contact your local bookseller or write to Special Markets, Fodor's Travel Publications, 201 East 50th Street, New York, NY 10022. Inquiries from Canada should be directed to your local Canadian bookseller or sent to Random House of Canada, Ltd., Marketing Department, 2775 Matheson Boulevard East, Mississauga, Ontario L4W 4P7. Inquiries from the United Kingdom should be sent to Fodor's Travel Publications, 20 Vauxhall Bridge Road, London SW1V 2SA, England.

PRINTED IN THE UNITED STATES OF AMERICA

10 9 8 7 6 5 4 3 2 1

CONTENTS

Maps

ON THE ROAD WITH FODOR'S

WHEN I PLAN A VA-CATION, the first thing I do is cast around among my friends and colleagues to find someone who's just been where I'm going. That's because there's no substitute for a recommendation from a good friend who knows your tastes, your budget, and your circumstances, someone who's just been there. Unfortunately, such friends are few and far between. So it's nice to know that there's *Fodor's Pocket Phoenix and Scottsdale.*

In the first place, this book won't stay home when you hit the road. It will accompany you every step of the way, steering you away from wrong turns and wrong choices and never expecting a thing in return. Most important, it's written and assiduously updated by the kind of people you *would* hit up for travel tips if you knew them. In these pages, they don't send you chasing down every sight but have instead selected the best ones, the ones that are worthy of your time and money. To make it easy for you to put it all together in the time you have, they've created half-day itineraries and neighborhood walks that you can mix and match in a snap.

About Our Writers

Our success in helping to make your trip the best of all possible vacations is a credit to the hard work of our extraordinary writers.

New York-based freelance writer **Rich Rubin** discovered Arizona when his parents bought a place in Scottsdale. He now travels there several times a year and has become, you might say, an addict.

Restaurant critic **Howard Seftel** has added an entirely new Phoenix dining section to this edition; not only is the section larger, but the coverage is wider, from Mexican taquerias to eclectic international bistros. Howard writes a popular restaurant column in the *New Times,* a weekly alternative newspaper in Phoenix.

Connections

We're pleased that the American Society of Travel Agents continues to endorse Fodor's as its guidebook of choice. ASTA is the world's largest and most influential travel trade association, operating in more than 170 countries, with 27,000 members pledged to adhere to a strict code of ethics reflecting the Society's motto, "Integrity in Travel." ASTA shares Fodor's devotion to providing smart, honest travel information and advice to travelers, and we've long recommended that our readers—even those who have guidebooks and traveling friends—consult ASTA member agents for the experience and professionalism they bring to your vacation planning.

On Fodor's Web site (www.fodors.com), check out the new Resource Center, an online companion to the Essential Information section of this book, complete with useful hot links to related sites. In our forums, you can also get lively advice from other travelers and more great tips from Fodor's experts worldwide.

How to Use This Book

Organization

Up front is **Essential Information,** an easy-to-use section arranged alphabetically by topic. Under each listing you'll find tips and information that will help you accomplish what you need to in Phoenix and Scottsdale. You'll also find addresses and telephone numbers of organizations and companies that offer destination-related services and detailed information and publications.

The first chapter in the guide, Destination: Phoenix and Scottsdale, helps get you in the mood for your trip. Pleasures and Pastimes describes the activities and sights that make metropolitan Phoenix

unique, Half-Day Itineraries targets the essential sights, and New and Noteworthy cues you in on the latest major developments.

The Exploring chapter is divided by neighborhood and town; each recommends a walking or driving tour and lists sights in alphabetical order. The remaining chapters are arranged in alphabetical order by subject (dining, lodging, nightlife and the arts, and shopping).

Icons and Symbols

★ Our special recommendation
✕ Restaurant
🏨 Lodging establishment
✕🏨 Lodging establishment whose restaurant warrants a special trip
🦆 Good for kids (rubber duck)
☞ Sends you to another section of the guide for more information
✉ Address
☎ Telephone number
☉ Opening and closing times
💶 Admission prices (those we give apply to adults; substantially reduced fees are almost always available for children, students, and senior citizens)

Numbers in white and black circles ③ ❸ that appear on the maps, in the margins, and within the tours correspond to one another.

Hotel Facilities

Unless otherwise noted, assume that the rooms in the lodgings reviewed have private baths and that the rates include no meals. If a lodging serves breakfast, we specify whether it is full or Continental in the italicized service information at the end of the review; if more than breakfast is served we specify whether the meal plan is the **Modified American Plan** (MAP, with breakfast and dinner daily), or the **Full American Plan** (FAP, with all meals).

Restaurant Reservations and Dress Codes

Reservations are always a good idea; we mention them only when they're essential or are not accepted. Book as far ahead as you can, and reconfirm as soon as you arrive. Unless otherwise noted, the restaurants listed are open daily for lunch and dinner. We mention dress only when men are required to wear a jacket or a jacket and tie.

Credit Cards

The following abbreviations are used: **AE**, American Express; **D**, Discover; **DC**, Diners Club; **MC**, MasterCard; and **V**, Visa.

Don't Forget to Write

You can use this book in the confidence that all prices and opening times are based on information supplied to us at press time; Fodor's cannot accept responsibility for any errors. Time inevitably brings changes, so always confirm information when it matters—especially if you're making a detour to visit a specific place.

Were the restaurants we recommended as described? Did our hotel picks exceed your expectations? Did you find a museum we recommended a waste of time? Keeping a travel guide fresh and up-to-date is a big job, and we welcome your feedback, positive and negative. If you have complaints, we'll look into them and revise our entries when the facts warrant it. If you've discovered a special place that we haven't included, we'll pass the information along to our correspondents and have them check it out. So send us your thoughts via e-mail at editors@fodors.com (specifying the name of the book on the subject line) or on paper in care of the Arizona editor at Fodor's, 201 East 50th Street, New York, New York 10022. In the meantime, have a wonderful trip!

Karen Cure
Editorial Director

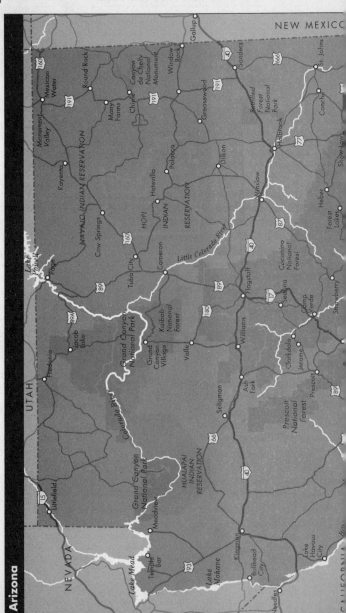

Arizona

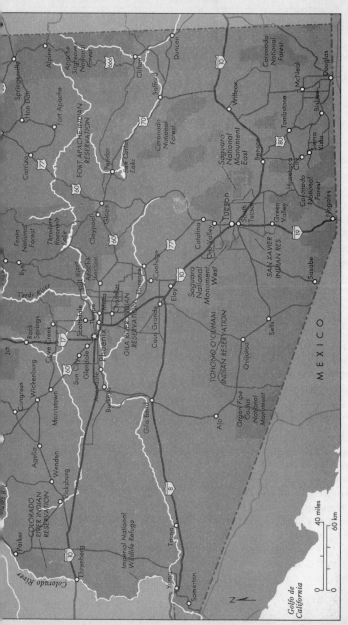

ESSENTIAL INFORMATION

Basic Information on Traveling in Phoenix and Scottsdale, Savvy Tips to Make Your Trip a Breeze, and Companies and Organizations to Contact

AIR TRAVEL

BOOKING YOUR FLIGHT

Price is just one factor to consider when booking a flight: frequency of service and even a carrier's safety record are often just as important. Major airlines offer the greatest number of departures. Smaller airlines—including regional and no-frills airlines—usually have a limited number of flights daily. On the other hand, so-called low-cost airlines usually are cheaper, and their fares impose fewer restrictions, such as advance-purchase requirements. Safety-wise, low-cost carriers as a group have a good history—about equal to that of major carriers.

When you book, **look for nonstop flights** and **remember that "direct" flights stop at least once.** Try to **avoid connecting flights,** which require a change of plane. Two airlines may jointly operate a connecting flight, so ask if your airline operates every segment— you may find that your preferred carrier flies you only part of the way.

CARRIERS

➤ MAJOR AIRLINES: **American** (☎ 800/433–7300). **America West** (☎ 800/235–9292). **Continental** (☎ 800/525–0280). **Delta** (☎ 800/221–1212). **Northwest** (☎ 800/225–2525). **TWA** (☎ 800/221–2000). **United** (☎ 800/241–6522). **US Airways** (☎ 800/428–4322).

➤ SMALLER AIRLINES: **Alaska Airlines** (☎ 800/426–0333). **America Trans Air** (☎ 800/225–2995). **Frontier Airlines** (☎ 800/432–1359). **Great Lakes Aviation** (☎ 800/274–0662). **Midwest Express** (☎ 800/452–2022. **Southwest** (☎ 800/435–9792). **Western Pacific** (☎ 800/930–3030).

➤ FROM THE U.K.: **American Airlines** (☎ 0345/789–789) from Heathrow via Chicago or from Gatwick via Dallas. **Continental Airlines** (☎ 0800/776–464 or 01293/776–464) from Gatwick via Houston and from Manchester via Newark. **Delta** (☎ 0800/414–767) flies from London's Gatwick Airport to Phoenix via Atlanta or Cincinnati.

➤ WITHIN ARIZONA: Within the state, **America West Express/ Mesa** (☎ 800/235–9292) operates regularly scheduled flights from Phoenix to Flagstaff, Prescott, Lake Havasu, Laughlin, Kingman, Sierra Vista, and Yuma. **Great Lakes Aviation** (☎ 800/ 274–0662) flies from Phoenix to Show Low and Page.

CHECK IN & BOARDING

The first passengers to get bumped are those who checked in late and those flying on discounted tickets, so **get to the gate and check in as early as possible,** especially during peak periods.

Always **bring a government-issued photo ID to the airport.** You may be asked to show it before you are allowed to check in.

CUTTING COSTS

The least-expensive airfares are priced for round-trip travel and usually must be purchased in advance. It's smart to **call a number of airlines, and when you are quoted a good price, book it on the spot**—the same fare may not be available the next day. Airlines generally allow you to change your return date for a fee. If you don't use your ticket, you can apply the cost toward the purchase of a new ticket, again for a small charge. However, most low-fare tickets are nonrefundable. To get the lowest airfare, **check different routings.** Compare prices of flights to and from different airports if your destination or home city has more than one gateway. Also price off-peak flights, which may be significantly less expensive.

When flying within the United States, **plan to stay over a Saturday night** and **travel during the middle of the week** to get the lowest fare. These low fares are usually priced for round-trip travel and are nonrefundable. You can, however, change your return date for a fee ($75 on most major airlines).

Travel agents, especially those who specialize in finding the lowest fares (☞ Discounts & Deals, *below*), can be especially helpful when booking a plane ticket. When you're quoted a price, **ask your agent if the price is likely to get any lower.** Good agents know the seasonal fluctuations of airfares and can usually anticipate a sale or fare war. However, waiting can be risky: the fare could go *up* as seats become scarce, and you may wait so long that your preferred flight sells out. A wait-and-see strategy works best if your plans are flexible. If you must arrive and depart on certain dates, don't delay.

FLYING TIMES

Flying time is 5½ hours from New York, 3½ hours from Chicago, and 1¼ hours from Los Angeles.

HOW TO COMPLAIN

If your baggage goes astray or your flight goes awry, complain right away. Most carriers require that you **file a claim immediately.**

➤ AIRLINE COMPLAINTS: U.S. Department of Transportation **Aviation Consumer Protection Division** (✉ C-75, Room 4107, Washington, DC 20590, ☎ 202/366–2220). **Federal Aviation Administration Consumer Hotline** (☎ 800/322–7873).

AIRPORTS

Phoenix Sky Harbor International is just 3 mi east of downtown Phoenix, and is surrounded by freeways linking it to almost every part of the metro area.

➤ AIRPORT INFORMATION: **Phoenix Sky Harbor International** (✉ 24th and Buckeye Sts., off I-10, ☎ 602/273–3300).

AIRPORT TO DOWNTOWN

You should definitely rent a car, either at the airport or wherever you are staying (most rental firms deliver). It's easy to get from Sky Harbor to downtown Phoenix (3 mi west) and Tempe (3 mi east) within 15 minutes. The airport is also only 20 minutes by freeway from Glendale (to the west) and Mesa (to the east). Scottsdale (to the northeast) can be reached via the Squaw Peak Parkway (AZ 51), but is a route of all surface streets (depending on destination, 44th Street from the Airport, then Camelback Road into Scottsdale is usually the easiest); both options take a half hour to 45 minutes by car, depending on traffic.

BY BUS

In about 20 minutes, **Valley Metro buses** (☎ 602/253–5000) will get you directly from Terminal 2, 3, or 4 to the bus terminal downtown (✉ 1st and Washington Sts.) or to Tempe (✉ Mill and University Aves.). With free transfers, the bus can take you from the airport to most other Valley cities (Glendale, Sun City, Scottsdale, etc.), but the trip is likely to be slow unless you take an express line. Fare is $1.25.

The **Red Line** runs westbound to Phoenix every half hour from about 6 AM until after 9 PM weekdays. Saturday, you take Bus 13 and transfer at Central Avenue to Bus 0 north; there is no Sunday service. The Red Line runs eastbound to Tempe every half hour from 3:30 AM to 7 PM weekdays (no weekend service); in another 25 minutes, it takes you to downtown Mesa (✉ Center and Main Sts.).

BY CAR

See Car Rental, *below,* which lists rental companies that have airport booths or free pickup from nearby lots.

BY SHUTTLE

Very few hotels offer a complimentary limo or shuttle, but most resorts do. The blue vans of **Supershuttle** (☎ 602/244–9000 or 800/258–3826) cruise Sky Harbor, each taking up to seven passengers to their individual destinations, with no luggage fee or airport surcharge. Wheelchair vans are also available. Drivers accept credit cards and expect tips.

BY TAXI AND LIMOUSINE
Only three taxi firms are licensed to pick up at Sky Harbor's commercial terminals. All add a $1 surcharge for airport pickups, do not charge for luggage, and are available 24 hours a day. A trip to downtown Phoenix can range from $6.50 to $12. The fare to downtown Scottsdale averages about $15–$16. A few limousine firms are allowed to cruise Sky Harbor, and many more provide airport pickups by reservation. All are on 24-hour call and charge about $3 for the first mile and $1.50 per mile thereafter. All expect tips.

➤ TAXI: **AAA Cab** (☎ 602/253–8294). **Checker/Yellow Cab** (☎ 602/252–5252). **Courier Cab** (☎ 602/232–2222).

➤ LIMOUSINE: **AAA Transportation** (☎ 602/242–3094) charges $15–$50, depending on distance. **Classic Limousine** (☎ 602/252–5166) will take up to six passengers (by reservation only) for $65, depending on how far you're going. **Scottsdale Limousine** (☎ 602/946–8446) also requires reservations but offers a toll-free number (☎ 800/747–8234); it costs from $40 to $70, plus tip.

BUS TRAVEL
Valley Metro (☎ 602/253–5000) has 21 express lines and 51 regular routes that reach most of the Valley suburbs. But there are no 24-hour routes; only a skeletal few lines run between sundown and 10:30 PM or on Saturday, and there is no Sunday service. Fares are $1.25 for regular service, $1.75 for express, with free transfers. The City of Phoenix also runs a 30¢ **Downtown Area Shuttle (DASH)**, with purple minibuses circling the area between the Arizona Center and the state capitol at 15-minute intervals. The system also serves major thoroughfares in several suburbs—Glendale, Scottsdale, Tempe, Mesa, and Chandler. The City of Tempe operates the **Free Local Area Shuttle (FLASH)**, which serves the downtown Tempe and Arizona State University area from 7 AM until 8 PM. In addition, **Dial-a-Ride** services (☎ 602/253–4000) are available throughout the Valley on Sundays.

LONG-DISTANCE BUS LINES
Greyhound (✉ 2115 E. Buckeye Rd., ☎ 602/389–4200 or 800/231–2222) has statewide and national routes to and from its main terminal near Sky Harbor airport.

CAMERAS & COMPUTERS
EQUIPMENT PRECAUTIONS
Always **keep your film, tape, or computer disks out of the sun.** Carry an extra supply of batteries, and **be prepared to turn on your camera, camcorder, or laptop** to prove to security personnel that the device is real. Always **ask for hand inspection of film,** which becomes clouded after successive exposure to airport X-ray machines,

and **keep videotapes and computer disks away from metal detectors.**

ON-LINE ON THE ROAD

Checking your E-mail or surfing the Web can sometimes be done in the business centers of major hotels, which usually charge an hourly rate. Web access is also available at many fax and copy centers, many of which are open 24 hours and on weekends. Whether you have E-mail at home or not, you can **arrange to have a free E-mail address** from several services, including one available at www.hotmail.com (the site explains how to apply for an address).

CAR RENTAL

To get around the metropolitan area, **you will need a car.** Downtown Phoenix and Scottsdale are pedestrian-friendly. There is no mass transit beyond a bus system that does not even run seven days a week. Tax on car rentals is 9.5%.

➤ MAJOR AGENCIES: **ABC** (☏ 888/899–9997). **Alamo** (☏ 800/ 327–9633, 0800/272–2000 in the U.K.). **Avis** (☏ 800/331– 1212, 800/879–2847 in Canada, 008/225–533 in Australia). **Budget** (☏ 800/527–0700, 0800/ 181181 in the U.K.). **Dollar** (☏ 800/800–4000, 0990/565656 in the U.K., where it is known as Eurodollar). **Enterprise** (☏ 800/ 829–1853). **Hertz** (☏ 800/654– 3131, 800/263–0600 in Canada, 0345/555888 in the U.K., 03/

9222–2523 in Australia, 03/358– 6777 in New Zealand). **National InterRent** (☏ 800/227–7368; 0345/222525 in the U.K., where it is known as Europcar Inter-Rent). If you care more about your wallet than about appearances, **Rent-a-Wreck** (☏ 602/ 252–4897 or 800/828–5975). **Thrifty** (☏ 800/367–2277).

CUTTING COSTS

To get the best deal, **book through a travel agent who is willing to shop around.** When pricing cars, **ask about the location of the rental lot.** Some off-airport locations offer lower rates, and their lots are only minutes from the terminal via complimentary shuttle. You also may want to **price local car-rental companies,** whose rates may be lower still, although their service and maintenance may not be as good as those of a name-brand agency. Remember to ask about required deposits, cancellation penalties, and drop-off charges if you're planning to pick up the car in one city and leave it in another.

Also **ask your travel agent about a company's customer-service record.** How has the company responded to late plane arrivals and vehicle mishaps? Are there often lines at the rental counter? If you're traveling during a holiday period, does a confirmed reservation guarantee you a car?

Be sure to **look into wholesalers,** companies that do not own fleets but rent in bulk from those that do and often offer better rates than traditional car-rental operations. Prices are best during off-peak periods.

➤ RENTAL WHOLESALERS: **Auto Europe** (☎ 207/842–2000 or 800/223–5555, FAX 800/235–6321). **Kemwel Holiday Autos** (☎ 914/835–5555 or 800/678–0678, FAX 914/835–5126).

INSURANCE

When driving a rented car you are generally responsible for any damage to or loss of the vehicle. You also are liable for any property damage or personal injury that you may cause while driving. Before you rent, **see what coverage you already have** under the terms of your personal auto-insurance policy and credit cards.

For about $15 to $20 per day, rental companies sell protection, known as a collision- or loss-damage waiver (CDW or LDW), that eliminates your liability for damage to the car; it's always optional and should never be automatically added to your bill.

In Arizona, the car-rental company must pay for damage to third parties up to a preset legal limit. Once that limit is reached, your personal auto or other liability insurance kicks in. However, **make sure you have enough coverage to pay for the car.** If you do not have auto insurance or an umbrella policy that covers damage

to third parties, purchasing liability insurance and a CDW or LDW is highly recommended.

REQUIREMENTS

In Arizona you must be 21 to rent a car, and rates may be higher if you're under 25. You'll pay extra for child seats (about $3 per day), which are compulsory for children under four, and for additional drivers (about $2 per day). Non-U.S. residents will need a reservation voucher, a passport, a driver's license, and a travel policy that covers each driver in order to pick up a car.

SURCHARGES

Before you pick up a car in one city and leave it in another, **ask about drop-off charges or one-way service fees,** which can be substantial. Note, too, that some rental agencies charge extra if you return the car before the time specified in your contract. To avoid a hefty refueling fee, **fill the tank just before you turn in the car,** but be aware that gas stations near the rental outlet may overcharge.

CAR TRAVEL

ARRIVING AND DEPARTING

Most highways into the state are good to excellent, with easy access, roadside facilities, rest stops, and scenic views. The speed limit on the freeways is now 75 mph, but **don't drive much faster than the limit**—police use sophisticated detection systems to catch violators.

You might pass through one or more of the state's 23 Native American reservations. Roads and other areas within reservation boundaries are under the jurisdiction of reservation police and governed by separate rules and regulations. **Observe all signs and respect Native Americans' privacy.** Be careful not to hit any animals, which often wander onto the roads; the penalties can be very high.

DRIVING IN PHOENIX AND SCOTTSDALE

Most metro-area streets are well marked and well lighted, and the freeway system is making gradual progress in linking Valley areas.

Around downtown Phoenix, AZ 202 (Papago Freeway), AZ 143 (Hohokam Freeway), and I–10 (Maricopa Freeway) make an elongated east–west loop, embracing the state capitol area to the west and Tempe to the east. At mid-loop, AZ 51 (Squaw Peak Freeway) runs north into Paradise Valley. And from the loop's east end, I–10 runs south to Tucson, 100 mi away (though it's still referred to as I–10 east, as it is eventually headed that way); U.S. 60 (Superstition Freeway) branches east to Tempe and Mesa.

Roads in Phoenix and its suburbs are laid out on a single, 800-square-mi grid. Even the freeways run predominantly north–south and east–west. (Grand Avenue,

running about 20 mi from northwest downtown to Sun City, is the *only* diagonal.)

Central Avenue is the main north–south grid axis: all roads parallel to and west of Central are numbered *avenues*; all roads parallel to and east of Central are numbered *streets*. The numbering begins at Central and increases in each direction.

Camera devices are mounted on several street lights to catch speeders and red light runners, and their location is constantly changing. You may return home only to find a ticket waiting for you. Smart commuters avoid Paradise Valley, where incomes may be sky high but speed limits are ridiculously low; and locals swear that Indian School is a better street than Camelback for driving between Phoenix and Scottsdale.

Weekdays, 6–9 AM and 4–6 PM, the center or left-turn lanes on the major surface arteries of 7th Street and 7th Avenue become one-way traffic-flow lanes between McDowell Road and Dunlap Avenue. These specially marked lanes are dedicated mornings to north–south traffic (into downtown) and afternoons to south–north traffic (out of downtown).

AUTO CLUBS

➤ IN AUSTRALIA: **Australian Automobile Association** (☎ 06/247–7311).

➤ IN CANADA: **Canadian Automobile Association** (CAA, ☎ 613/247–0117).

➤ IN NEW ZEALAND: **New Zealand Automobile Association** (☎ 09/377–4660).

➤ IN THE U.K.: **Automobile Association** (AA, ☎ 0990/500–600), **Royal Automobile Club** (RAC, ☎ 0990/722–722 for membership, 0345/121–345 for insurance).

➤ IN THE U.S.: **American Automobile Association** (☎ 800/222–4357).

EMERGENCY SERVICES

Dial 911 to report accidents on the road and to reach police, the Arizona Highway Patrol, or fire department.

GASOLINE

At press time, regular unleaded gasoline at self-serve stations costs about $1.25 a gallon.

ROAD CONDITIONS

The highways in Arizona are well maintained, but if you'll be driving through the state, be aware of dust storms, flash floods, and desert heat. **Arizona Road and Weather Conditions Service** (☎ 602/651–2400, ext. 7623) can provide current information.

RULES OF THE ROAD

In the cities, freeway limits are between 55 and 65 mph. Arizona requires seat belts on front-seat passengers and children 16 and under. Tickets can be given for failing to comply. Children under age four must be in child safety seats. Unless otherwise indicated, right turns are allowed on red lights after you've come to a full stop, and left turns onto adjoining one-way streets are allowed on red lights after you've come to a full stop. Driving with a blood-alcohol level higher than 0.10 will result in arrest and seizure of driver license. Fines are severe.

CHILDREN & TRAVEL

CHILDREN IN PHOENIX AND SCOTTSDALE

Many large resorts have special activities for children, and many offer baby-sitting services.

➤ LOCAL INFORMATION: The monthly magazine *Raising Arizona Kids* focuses on Phoenix happenings and includes a calendar of children-friendly events around the state. You can buy single copies for $1.95 each at Borders, L'il Things, and Smith stores in Tucson and Phoenix, or send $24.95 for a year's subscription (⊠ 2445 E. Shea Blvd., Suite 201, Phoenix 85028, ☎ 602/953–KIDS or in Arizona 888/RAISING, ℻ 602/953–3305).

HOTELS

Most hotels in Arizona allow children under a certain age to stay in their parents' room at no extra charge, but others charge them as extra adults; be sure to **ask about the cutoff age for children's discounts.**

All **Holiday Inns** allow children under age 19 to stay free when sharing a room with an adult. The **Pointe Hilton Resort at Squaw Peak** runs its Coyote Camp for children ages 4–12 year-round. The **Phoenician Resort** in Scottsdale has junior golf and tennis clinics for kids 5–14 throughout the year; Scottsdale's **Hyatt Regency** also offers a full range of supervised daytime activities geared for kids 3–12. All of the above resorts also have baby-sitting services.

➤ BEST CHOICES: Holiday Inns (☎ 800/465–4329). Westin La Paloma Hotel (☎ 800/228–3000). Tanque Verde Guest Ranch (☎ 800/234–3833). Pointe Hilton Resort at Squaw Peak (☎ 800/934–1000). Phoenician Resort (☎ 800/888–8234). Hyatt Regency (☎ 800/233–1234).

CONSUMER PROTECTION

Whenever possible, **pay with a major credit card** so you can cancel payment or get reimbursed if there's a problem, provided that you can provide documentation. This is the best way to pay, whether you're buying travel arrangements before your trip or shopping at your destination.

If you're doing business with a particular company for the first time, **contact your local Better Business Bureau and the attorney general's offices** in your state and the company's home state, as well. Have any complaints been filed?

Finally, if you're buying a package or tour, always **consider travel insurance** that includes default coverage (☞ Insurance, *below*).

➤ LOCAL BBBs: **Council of Better Business Bureaus** (✉ 4200 Wilson Blvd., Suite 800, Arlington, VA 22203, ☎ 703/276–0100, FAX 703/525–8277).

CUSTOMS & DUTIES

When shopping, **keep receipts** for all of your purchases. Upon reentering your country, **be ready to show customs officials what you've bought.**

IN AUSTRALIA

Australia residents who are 18 or older may bring back $A400 worth of souvenirs and gifts (including jewelry), 250 cigarettes or 250 grams of tobacco, and 1,125 milliliters of alcohol (including wine, beer, and spirits). Residents under 18 may bring back $A200 worth of goods.

➤ INFORMATION: **Australian Customs Service** (Regional Director, ✉ Box 8, Sydney, NSW 2001, ☎ 02/9213–2000, FAX 02/9213–4000).

IN CANADA

Canadian residents who have been out of Canada for at least seven days may bring in C$500 worth of goods duty-free. If you've been away less than seven days but more than 48 hours, the duty-free allowance drops to C$200; if your trip lasts 24–48 hours, the allowance is C$50. You may not pool allowances with family members. Goods claimed under the C$500 exemption may follow you by mail; those claimed under the lesser exemptions must accompany you. Alcohol and tobacco products may be included in the seven-day and 48-hour exemptions but not in the 24-hour exemption. If you meet the age requirements of the province or territory through which you reenter Canada, you may bring in, duty-free, 1.14 liters (40 imperial ounces) of wine or liquor *or* 24 12-ounce cans or bottles of beer or ale. If you are 16 or older you may bring in, duty-free, 200 cigarettes and 50 cigars.

You may send an unlimited number of gifts worth up to C$60 each duty-free to Canada. Label the package UNSOLICITED GIFT—VALUE UNDER $60. Alcohol and tobacco are excluded.

➤ INFORMATION: **Revenue Canada** (✉ 2265 St. Laurent Blvd. S, Ottawa, Ontario K1G 4K3, ☎ 613/993–0534, 800/461–9999 in Canada).

IN NEW ZEALAND

Homeward-bound residents with goods to declare must present themselves for inspection. If you're 17 or older, you may bring back $700 worth of souvenirs and gifts. Your duty-free allowance also includes 4.5 liters of wine or beer; one 1,125-milliliter bottle of spirits; and either 200 cigarettes, 250 grams of tobacco, 50 cigars, or a combo of all three up to 250 grams.

➤ INFORMATION: **New Zealand Customs** (✉ Custom House, 50 Anzac Ave., Box 29, Auckland, New Zealand, ☎ 09/359–6655, ☎ 09/309–2978).

IN THE U.K.

From countries outside the EU, including the United States, you may import, duty-free, 200 cigarettes or 50 cigars; 1 liter of spirits or 2 liters of fortified or sparkling wine or liqueurs; 2 liters of still table wine; 60 milliliters of perfume; 250 milliliters of toilet water; plus £136 worth of other goods, including gifts and souvenirs.

➤ INFORMATION: **HM Customs and Excise** (✉ Dorset House, Stamford St., London SE1 9NG, ☎ 0171/202–4227).

DISABILITIES & ACCESSIBILITY

ACCESS IN ARIZONA

➤ LOCAL RESOURCES: **Southern Arizona Group Office** (☎ 602/640–5250) for information on accessible facilities at specific parks and sites in Arizona.

MAKING RESERVATIONS

When discussing accessibility with an operator or reservations agent, **ask hard questions.** Are there any stairs, inside *or* out? Are there grab bars next to the toilet *and* in the shower/tub? How wide is the doorway to the room? To the bathroom? For the most extensive facilities meeting the latest legal specifications, **opt for newer accommodations,** which are more likely to have been designed with access in mind. Be sure to **discuss your needs before booking.**

TRANSPORTATION

➤ Bus: Greyhound (☎ 800/752–4841; TTY 800/345–3109), which provides service to many destinations in Arizona, will carry a person with disabilities and a companion for the price of a single fare.

➤ Car: **Avis** (☎ 800/331–1212), **Hertz** (☎ 800/654–3131), and **National** (☎ 800/328–4567) can provide hand controls on some rental cars with advance notice.

➤ Train: **Amtrak** (✉ National Railroad Passenger Corp., 60 Massachusetts Ave. NE, Washington, DC 20002, ☎ 800/872–7245) advises that you request redcap service, special seats, or wheelchair assistance when you make reservations. Also note that not all stations are equipped to provide these services. All passengers with disabilities are entitled to a 15% discount on the lowest fare, and there are special fares for children with disabilities as well. Contact Amtrak for a free brochure that outlines services for older travelers and people with disabilities.

TRAVEL AGENCIES & TOUR OPERATORS

As a whole, the travel industry has become more aware of the needs of travelers with disabilities. In the United States, the Americans with Disabilities Act requires that travel firms serve the needs of all travelers. Note, though, that some agencies and operators specialize in making travel arrangements for individuals and groups with disabilities.

➤ Travelers with Mobility Problems: **Access Adventures** (✉ 206 Chestnut Ridge Rd., Rochester, NY 14624, ☎ 716/889–9096), run by a former physical-rehabilitation counselor. **Accessible Journeys** (✉ 35 W. Sellers Ave., Ridley Park, PA 19078, ☎ 610/521–0339 or 800/846–4537, FAX 610/521–6959), for escorted tours exclusively for travelers with mobility impairments. **Flying Wheels Travel** (✉ 143 W. Bridge St., Box 382, Owatonna, MN 55060, ☎ 507/451–5005 or 800/535–6790, FAX 507/451–1685), a travel agency specializing in customized tours and itineraries worldwide. **Hinsdale Travel Service** (✉ 201 E. Ogden Ave., Suite 100, Hinsdale, IL 60521, ☎ 630/325–1335), a travel agency that benefits from the advice of wheelchair traveler Janice Perkins.

DISCOUNTS & DEALS

CLUBS & COUPONS

Many companies sell discounts in the form of travel clubs and coupon books, but these cost money. You must use participating advertisers to get a deal, and only after you recoup the initial membership cost or book price do you begin to save. If you plan to use the club or coupons frequently, you may save considerably. Before signing up, find out what discounts you get for free.

➤ DISCOUNT CLUBS: **Entertainment Travel Editions** (⊠ 2125 Butterfield Rd., Troy, MI 48084, ☎ 800/445–4137; $20–$51, depending on destination). **Great American Traveler** (⊠ Box 27965, Salt Lake City, UT 84127, ☎ 801/974–3033 or 800/548–2812; $49.95 per year). **Moment's Notice Discount Travel Club** (⊠ 7301 New Utrecht Ave., Brooklyn, NY 11204, ☎ 718/234–6295; $25 per year, single or family). **Privilege Card International** (⊠ 237 E. Front St., Youngstown, OH 44503, ☎ 330/746–5211 or 800/236–9732; $74.95 per year). **Sears's Mature Outlook** (⊠ Box 9390, Des Moines, IA 50306, ☎ 800/336–6330; $19.95 per year). **Travelers Advantage** (⊠ CUC Travel Service, 3033 S. Parker Rd., Suite 1000, Aurora, CO 80014, ☎ 800/548–1116 or 800/648–4037; $59.95 per year, single or family). **Worldwide Discount Travel Club** (⊠ 1674 Meridian Ave., Miami Beach, FL 33139, ☎ 305/534–2082; $50 per year family, $40 single).

CREDIT-CARD BENEFITS

When you use your credit card to make travel purchases you may get free travel-accident insurance, collision-damage insurance, and medical or legal assistance, depending on the card and the bank that issued it. American Express, MasterCard, and Visa provide one or more of these services, so **get a copy of your credit card's travel-benefits policy.** If you are a member of an auto club, always **ask hotel and car-rental reservations agents about auto-club discounts.** Some clubs offer additional discounts on tours, cruises, and admission to attractions.

DISCOUNT RESERVATIONS

To save money, **look into discount-reservations services** with toll-free numbers, which use their buying power to get a better price on hotels, airline tickets, even car rentals. When booking a room, always **call the hotel's local toll-free number** (if one is available) rather than the central reservations number—you'll often get a better price. Always ask about special packages or corporate rates.

➤ AIRLINE TICKETS: ☎ **800/FLY–4–LESS.** ☎ **800/FLY–ASAP.**

➤ HOTEL ROOMS: **RMC Travel** (☎ 800/245–5738).

EMERGENCIES

Police, fire, ambulance, or highway emergencies (☎ 911). The **Poison Control Center** (☎ 602/253–3334).

GAY & LESBIAN TRAVEL

There are no state-wide gay and lesbian oriented travel organizations in Arizona. When planning your trip, check out *Fodor's Gay Guide to the USA* (**Fodor's Travel Publications**, ☎ 800/533–6478 or in bookstores); $20.

➤ LOCAL PUBLICATIONS: *Heatstroke* (☎ 602/264–3646) is a Phoenix-based biweekly. The weekly *Observer* (☎ 520/622–7176) covers Tucson and Phoenix area.

GUIDED TOURS

Reservations for tours are a must all year, with seats often filling up quickly in the busy season, October–April. All tours provide pickup services at area resorts, but some offer lower prices if you drive to the tour's point of origin. For various outdoor excursions, *see* Chapter 6.

ORIENTATION TOURS

Gray Line Tours (✉ Box 21126, Phoenix 85036, ☎ 602/495–9100 or 800/732–0327) gives seasonal, three-hour narrated tours including downtown Phoenix, the Arizona Biltmore hotel, Camelback Mountain, mansions in Paradise Valley, Arizona State University, Papago Park, and Scottsdale's Old Town; the price is about $27.

Open Road Tours (✉ 748 E. Dunlap, No. 2, Phoenix 85020, ☎ 602/997–6474 or 800/766–7117) offers excursions to Sedona and the Grand Canyon, Phoenix city tours, and Native American–culture trips to the Salt River Pima Indian reservation.

Vaughan's Southwest Custom Tours (✉ Box 31312, Phoenix 85046, ☎ 602/971–1381 or 800/513–1381) gives a 4½-hour city tour for 11 or fewer passengers in custom vans, stopping at the Heard Museum, the Arizona Biltmore, and the state capitol building; the cost is $35. Vaughan's will also take visitors east of Phoenix on the Apache Trail. The tour is offered on Tuesday and Saturday, September–May; the cost is $60.

SPECIAL-INTEREST TOURS

Arizona Scenic Tours (✉ 2801 E. Victor Hugo Ave., Phoenix 85032, ☎ 602/971–3601) heads past Pinnacle Peak toward the Verde River on dirt desert roads. Two people can expect to pay $50 each (beverages included) for four hours.

Cimarron Adventures and River Co. (✉ 7714 E. Catalina Dr., Scottsdale 85251, ☎ 602/994–1199) arranges half-day float trips down the Salt, Verde, and Gila rivers. Trips cost about $55 per person.

Arizona Carriage Company (✉ 7319 E. Second St., Scottsdale 85251, ☎ 602/423–1449) leads 15-minute to one-hour horse-drawn-carriage tours around Old Scottsdale for $20–$70.

WALKING TOUR

A 45-minute self-guided walking tour of Old Scottsdale takes visitors to 14 historic sites in the area. Maps showing the route can be picked up in the **Scottsdale Chamber of Commerce** (☞ Visitor Information, *below*).

HEALTH

➤ DOCTORS AND DENTISTS: The **Maricopa County Medical Society** (☎ 602/252–2844) and the **Arizona Osteopathic Medical Association** (☎ 602/840–0460) offer referrals during business hours on weekdays. The **American Dental Association Valley chapter** (☎ 602/957–4864) has a 24-hour referral hot line.

➤ HOSPITALS: **Samaritan Health Service** (☎ 602/230–2273) has four Valley hospitals—Good Samaritan (downtown), Desert Samaritan (east), Maryvale Samaritan (southwest), and Thunderbird Samaritan (northwest)—and a west Valley urgent-care clinic; all share a 24-hour hot line. **Scottsdale Memorial Hospital** (☎ 602/481–4000 or 602/860–3000) has two campuses in the northeastern valley. **Maricopa County Medical Center** (☎ 602/267–5011) has been rated one of the nation's best public hospitals.

MEDICAL PLANS

No one plans to get sick while traveling, but it happens, so **consider signing up with a medical-assistance company.** Members get doctor referrals, emergency evacuation or repatriation, 24-hour telephone hot lines for medical consultation, cash for emergencies, and other personal and legal assistance. Coverage varies by plan, so **review the benefits of each carefully.**

➤ MEDICAL-ASSISTANCE COMPANIES: **International SOS Assistance** (✉ 8 Neshaminy Interplex, Suite 207, Trevose, PA 19053, ☎ 215/245–4707 or 800/523–6586, ℻ 215/244–9617; ✉ 12 Chemin Riantbosson, 1217 Meyrin 1, Geneva, Switzerland, ☎ 4122/785–6464, ℻ 4122/785–6424; ✉ 10 Anson Rd., 14-07/08 International Plaza, Singapore 079903, ☎ 65/226–3936, ℻ 65/226–3937).

INSURANCE

Travel insurance is the best way to **protect yourself against financial loss.** The most useful plan is a comprehensive policy that includes coverage for trip cancellation and interruption, default, trip delay, and medical expenses (with a waiver for preexisting conditions).

Without insurance, you will lose all or most of your money if you cancel your trip, regardless of the reason. Default insurance covers you if your tour operator, airline, or cruise line goes out of business. Trip-delay covers unforeseen expenses that you may incur due to bad weather or mechanical delays.

It's important to compare the fine print regarding trip-delay coverage when comparing policies.

For overseas travel, one of the most important components of travel insurance is its medical coverage. Supplemental health insurance will pick up the cost of your medical bills should you get sick or injured while traveling. Residents of the United Kingdom can buy an annual travel-insurance policy valid for most vacations taken during the year in which the coverage is purchased. If you are pregnant or have a preexisting condition, make sure you're covered. British citizens should buy extra medical coverage when traveling overseas, according to the Association of British Insurers. Australian travelers should buy travel insurance, including extra medical coverage, whenever they go abroad, according to the Insurance Council of Australia.

Always **buy travel insurance directly from the insurance company**; if you buy it from a cruise line, airline, or tour operator that goes out of business you probably will not be covered for the agency or operator's default, a major risk. Before you make any purchase, **review your existing health and homeowner's policies** to find out whether they cover expenses incurred while traveling.

➤ TRAVEL INSURERS: In the U.S., **Access America** (✉ 6600 W. Broad St., Richmond, VA 23230, ☎ 804/285–3300 or 800/284–8300). **Travel Guard International** (✉ 1145 Clark St., Stevens Point, WI 54481, ☎ 715/345–0505 or 800/826–1300). In Canada, **Mutual of Omaha** (✉ Travel Division, 500 University Ave., Toronto, Ontario M5G 1V8, ☎ 416/598–4083, 800/268–8825 in Canada).

➤ INSURANCE INFORMATION: In the U.K., **Association of British Insurers** (✉ 51 Gresham St., London EC2V 7HQ, ☎ 0171/600–3333). In Australia, the **Insurance Council of Australia** (☎ 613/9614–1077, FAX 613/9614–7924).

LODGING

APARTMENT & VILLA RENTALS

If you want a home base that's roomy enough for a family and comes with cooking facilities, **consider a furnished rental.** These can save you money, especially if you're traveling with a large group of people. Home-exchange directories list rentals (often second homes owned by prospective house swappers), and some services search for a house or apartment for you and handle the paperwork. Up-front registration fees may apply.

➤ RENTAL AGENTS: **Property Rentals International** (✉ 1008 Mansfield Crossing Rd., Richmond, VA 23236, ☎ 804/378–6054 or 800/220–3332, FAX 804/379–2073). **Rent-a-Home**

International (✉ 7200 34th
Ave. NW, Seattle, WA 98117,
☎ 206/789–9377 or 800/488–
7368, FAX 206/789–9379). **Hide-
aways International** (✉ 767
Islington St., Portsmouth, NH
03801, ☎ 603/430–4433 or 800/
843–4433, FAX 603/430–4444;
membership $99) is a club for
travelers who arrange rentals
among themselves.

BED & BREAKFASTS

➤ RESERVATION SERVICES: **Arizona
Association of Bed and Breakfast
Inns** (✉ Box 7186, Phoenix
85012, ☎ 800/284–2589). **Bed &
Breakfast Southwest** (✉ 2916 N.
70th St., Scottsdale 85251, ☎
602/995–2831 or 800/762–9704;
602/874–1316 outside AZ). **Mi
Casa Su Casa** (✉ Box 950, Tempe
85280, ☎ 602/990–0682 or 800/
456–0682, FAX 602/990–3390;
www.mi-casa.org). The Arizona
Office of Tourism (☞ Visitor Information, *below*) has a statewide
list of bed-and-breakfasts.

HOTELS

Most hotels will hold your reservation until 6 PM; **call ahead if you
plan to arrive late.** Hotels will be
more willing to hold a late reservation for you if you reserve with
a credit-card number.

When you call to make a reservation, **ask all the necessary questions up front.** If you are arriving
with a car, ask if the hotel has a
parking lot or covered garage and
whether there is an extra fee for
parking. If you like to eat your
meals in, ask if the hotel has a
restaurant or whether it has room
service (most do, but not necessar-
ily 24 hours a day—and be fore-
warned that it can be expensive).
Most hotels have in-room telephones, but double-check this at
inexpensive properties and bed-
and-breakfasts. Most hotels and
motels have in-room TVs, often
with cable movies (usually pay-
per-view), but verify this if you like
to watch TV. If you want an in-
room crib for your child, there will
probably be an additional charge.

MONEY

CREDIT & DEBIT CARDS

A credit card allows you to delay
payment and gives you certain
rights as a consumer (☞ Consumer Protection, *above*). A debit
card, also known as a check card,
deducts funds directly from your
checking account and helps you
stay within your budget. When
you want to rent a car, though,
you may still need an old-fash-
ioned credit card. Although you
can always *pay* for your car with
a debit card, some agencies will
not allow you to *reserve* a car
with a debit card.

Otherwise, the two types of plastic
are virtually the same. Both will
get you cash advances at ATMs
worldwide if your card is properly
programmed with your personal
identification number (PIN).

➤ ATM LOCATIONS: **Cirrus** (☎ 800/424–7787). **Plus** (☎ 800/843–7587) for locations in the U.S. and Canada, or visit your local bank.

➤ REPORTING LOST CARDS: To report lost or stolen credit cards, call the following toll-free numbers: **American Express** (☎ 800/327–2177); **Discover Card** (☎ 800/347–2683); **Diners Club** (☎ 800/234–6377); **Master Card** (☎ 800/307–7309); and **Visa** (☎ 800/847–2911).

TRAVELER'S CHECKS

Lost or stolen checks can usually be replaced within 24 hours. To ensure a speedy refund, buy your own traveler's checks—don't let someone else pay for them: irregularities like this can cause delays. The person who bought the checks should make the call to request a refund.

OPENING AND CLOSING TIMES

Generally, banks are open Monday–Thursday 9–4, Friday 9–6. Selected banks have Saturday-morning hours, and a few large grocery stores have bank windows that stay open until 9 PM. Most enclosed shopping malls are open weekdays 10–9, Saturday 10–6, and Sunday noon–5; some of the major centers are open later on weekends. Many grocery stores are open 7 AM–9 PM, but several major chain stores throughout the Valley are open 24 hours.

PACKING

LUGGAGE

How many carry-on bags you can bring with you is up to the airline. Most allow two, but the limit is often reduced to one on certain flights. Gate agents will take excess baggage—including bags they deem oversize—from you as you board and add it to checked luggage. To avoid this situation, make sure that everything you carry aboard will fit under your seat. Also, get to the gate early, and request a seat at the back of the plane; you'll probably board first, while the overhead bins are still empty.

Airline liability for baggage is limited to $1,250 per person on flights within the United States.

Before departure, **itemize your bags' contents** and their worth, and label the bags with your name, address, and phone number. (If you use your home address, cover it so that potential thieves can't see it readily.) Inside each bag, **pack a copy of your itinerary.** At check-in, **make sure that each bag is correctly tagged** with the destination airport's three-letter code. If your bags arrive damaged or fail to arrive at all, file a written report with the airline before leaving the airport.

PACKING LIST

Wear casual clothing and resort wear in Arizona. When in more elegant restaurants, as well as in dining rooms of some resorts, most men wear jackets and appropriate pants (few places require ties). Dressy casual wear is appropriate for women even in the nicest places—take along a silky blouse and chunky silver jewelry and you'll fit in almost anywhere.

Stay cool in cotton fabrics and light colors. T-shirts, polo shirts, sundresses, and lightweight shorts, trousers, skirts, and blouses are useful year-round in the south. **Bring sun hats, swimsuits, sandals, and sunscreen**—mandatory warm-weather items. And **don't forget jeans and sneakers or sturdy walking shoes**; they're important year-round.

Take along appropriate sports gear, although tennis, golf, and horseback-riding equipment is readily available for rental.

PASSPORTS & VISAS

When traveling internationally, make **two photocopies of the data page** (one for someone at home and another for you, carried separately from your passport). If you lose your passport, promptly call the nearest embassy or consulate and the local police.

➤ U.K. CITIZENS: **U.S. Embassy Visa Information Line** (☎ 01891/200–290; calls cost 49p per minute, 39p per minute cheap rate), for U.S. visa information. **U.S. Embassy Visa Branch** (✉ 5 Upper Grosvenor St., London W1A 2JB), for U.S. visa informa-

tion; send a self-addressed, stamped envelope. Write the **U.S. Consulate General** (✉ Queen's House, Queen St., Belfast BTI 6EO) if you live in Northern Ireland.

PASSPORT OFFICES

The best time to apply for a passport or to renew is during the fall and winter. Before any trip, be sure to check your passport's expiration date and, if necessary, renew it as soon as possible.

➤ AUSTRALIAN CITIZENS: **Australian Passport Office** (☎ 131–232).

➤ NEW ZEALAND CITIZENS: **New Zealand Passport Office** (☎ 04/494–0700 for information on how to apply, 0800/727–776 for information on applications already submitted).

➤ U.K. CITIZENS: **London Passport Office** (☎ 0990/21010), for fees and documentation requirements and to request an emergency passport.

RADIO STATIONS

AM

KTAR 620: news, talk, sports. **KFYI 910:** news, talk. **KOOL 960:** oldies. **KISO 1230:** adult contemporary. **KOPA 1440:** classic rock. **KPHX 1480:** Spanish-language.

FM

KBAQ 89.5: classical. **KJZZ 91.5:** acoustic jazz, National Public Radio. **KKFR 92.3:** contemporary hits. **KOOL 94.5:** oldies. **KGLQ**

96.9: classic hits. **KSLX 100.7:** classic rock. **KZON 101.5:** alternative rock. **KNIX 102.5:** country. **KEDJ 106.3:** alternative rock. **KVVA 107.1:** Spanish-language.

SENIOR-CITIZEN TRAVEL

To qualify for age-related discounts, **mention your senior-citizen status up front** when booking hotel reservations (not when checking out) and before you're seated in restaurants (not when paying the bill). Note that discounts may be limited to certain menus, days, or hours. When renting a car, **ask about promotional car-rental discounts,** which can be cheaper than senior-citizen rates.

➤ EDUCATIONAL PROGRAMS: **Elderhostel** (✉ 75 Federal St., 3rd floor, Boston, MA 02110, ☎ 617/426–8056).

TAXIS

Taxi fares are unregulated in Phoenix, except at the airport. (For a listing of leading firms and their fares, *see* Airport to Downtown, *above*.) The 800-square-mi metro area is so large that one-way fares in excess of $50 are not uncommon; you might want to ask what the damages will be before you get in. Except within a compact area, such as central Phoenix, travel by taxi is not recommended.

TELEPHONES

CREDIT-CARD CALLS

U.S. telephone credit cards are not like the magnetic cards used in some European countries, which pay for calls in advance; they simply represent an account that lets you charge a call to your home or business phone. On any phone, you can make a credit-card call by punching in your individual account number or by telling the operator that number. Certain specially marked pay phones (usually found in airports, hotel lobbies, and so on) can be used only for credit-card calls. To get a credit card, contact your long-distance telephone carrier, such as AT&T, MCI, or Sprint.

DIRECTORY & OPERATOR INFORMATION

For assistance from an operator, dial "0". To find out a telephone number, look in the phone book or call directory assistance at "411" for numbers within the area code, "555–1212" for numbers outside your area code. These calls are free even from a pay phone. If you want to charge a long-distance call to the person you're calling, you can call collect by dialing "0" instead of "1" before the 10-digit number, and an operator will come on the line to assist you (the party you're calling, however, has the right to refuse the call).

INTERNATIONAL CALLS

International calls can be direct-dialed from most phones; dial "011," followed by the country code and then the local number (the front pages of many local telephone directories include a list of overseas country codes). To have an operator assist you, dial "0" and ask for the overseas operator. The country code for Australia is 61; New Zealand, 64; and the United Kingdom, 44. To reach Canada, dial 1 + area code + number.

LONG-DISTANCE CALLS

Competitive long-distance carriers make calling within the United States relatively convenient and let you avoid hotel surcharges. By dialing an 800 number, you can get connected to the long-distance company of your choice.

➤ LONG-DISTANCE CARRIERS: **AT&T** (☎ 800/225–5288). **MCI** (☎ 800/888–8000). **Sprint** (☎ 800/366–2255).

PUBLIC PHONES

Instructions for pay telephones should be posted on the phone, but generally you insert your coins—35¢ for a local call—in a slot and wait for the steady hum of a dial tone before dialing the number you wish to reach. If you dial a long-distance number, the operator will come on the line and tell you how much more money you must insert for your call to go through.

TIME

Arizona sets its clocks to mountain standard time—two hours earlier than eastern standard, one hour later than Pacific standard.

However, from April to October, when other states switch to daylight saving time, Arizona does *not* change its clocks; during this portion of the year, the mountain standard hour in Arizona is the same as the Pacific daylight hour in California.

TIPPING

At restaurants, a 15% tip is standard for waiters; up to 20% may be expected at more expensive establishments. The same goes for taxi drivers, bartenders, and hairdressers. Coat-check operators usually expect $1; bellhops and porters should get 50¢ to $1 per bag; hotel maids in upscale hotels should get about $1 per day of your stay. For local sightseeing tours, you may individually tip the driver-guide $1 if he or she has been helpful or informative. Ushers in theaters do not expect tips.

TOUR OPERATORS

Buying a prepackaged tour or independent vacation can make your trip less expensive and more hassle-free. Because everything is prearranged, you'll spend less time planning.

Operators that handle several hundred thousand travelers per year can use their purchasing power to give you a good price. Their high volume may also indicate financial stability. But some small companies provide more personalized service; because they tend to specialize, they may also be more knowledgeable about a given area.

BOOKING WITH AN AGENT

Travel agents are excellent resources. In fact, large operators accept bookings made only through travel agents. But it's a good idea to **collect brochures from several agencies,** because some agents' suggestions may be influenced by relationships with tour and package firms that reward them for volume sales. If you have a special interest, **find an agent with expertise in that area**; ASTA (☞ Travel Agencies, *below*) has a database of specialists worldwide.

Make sure your travel agent knows the accommodations and other services. Ask about the hotel's location, room size, beds, and whether it has a pool, room service, or programs for children, if you care about these. Has your agent been there in person or sent others you can contact?

Do some homework on your own, too: local tourism boards can provide information about lesser-known and small-niche operators, some of which may sell only direct.

BUYER BEWARE

Each year consumers are stranded or lose their money when tour operators—even very large ones with excellent reputations—go out of business. So **check out the operator.** Find out how long the company has been in business, and ask

several travel agents about its reputation. If the package or tour you are considering is priced lower than in your wildest dreams, **be skeptical.** Try to **book with a company that has a consumer-protection program.** If the operator has such a program, you'll find information about it in the company's brochure. If the operator you are considering does not offer some kind of consumer protection, then ask for references from satisfied customers.

In the United States, members of the National Tour Association and United States Tour Operators Association are required to set aside funds to cover your payments and travel arrangements in case the company defaults. It's also a good idea to choose a company that participates in the American Society of Travel Agent's Tour Operator Program (TOP). This gives you a forum if there are any disputes between you and your tour operator; ASTA will act as mediator.

➤ TOUR-OPERATOR RECOMMENDATIONS: **American Society of Travel Agents** (☞ Travel Agencies, *below*). **National Tour Association** (✉ NTA, ✉ 546 E. Main St., Lexington, KY 40508, ☎ 606/ 226–4444 or 800/755–8687). **United States Tour Operators Association** (✉ USTOA, ✉ 342 Madison Ave.; Suite 1522, New York, NY 10173, ☎ 212/599– 6599 or 800/468–7862, FAX 212/ 599–6744).

COSTS

The more your package or tour includes, the better you can predict the ultimate cost of your vacation. Make sure you know exactly what is covered, and **beware of hidden costs.** Are taxes, tips, and service charges included? Transfers and baggage handling? Entertainment and excursions? These can add up.

PACKAGES

Independent vacation packages are available from major tour operators and airlines. The companies listed below offer vacation packages in a broad price range.

➤ AIR/HOTEL/CAR: **Certified Vacations** (✉ Box 1525, Fort Lauderdale, FL 33302, ☎ 305/522–1414 or 800/233–7260). **Delta Vacations** (☎ 800/872–7786). **Globetrotters** (✉ 139 Main St., Cambridge, MA 02142, ☎ 617/621–0099 or 800/333–1234). **TWA Getaway Vacations** (☎ 800/438–2929). **United Vacations** (☎ 800/328–6877). **US Airways Vacations** (☎ 800/455–0123).

➤ CUSTOM PACKAGES: **Amtrak Vacations** (☎ 800/321–8684).

➤ FROM THE U.K.: **British Airways Holidays** (✉ Astral Towers, Betts Way, London Rd., Crawley, West Sussex RH10 2XA, ☎ 01293/723–121). **Jetsave Travel Ltd.** (✉ Sussex House, London Rd., East Grinstead, West Sussex RH19 1LD, ☎ 01342/327–711). **Key to America** (✉ 1–3 Station Rd., Ashford, Middlesex TW15 2UW, ☎ 01784/248–777). **Kuoni Travel** (✉ Kuoni House, Dorking, Surrey RH5 4AZ, ☎ 01306/740–500). **Premier Holidays** (✉ Premier Travel Centre, Westbrook, Milton Rd., Cambridge CB4 1YG, ☎ 01223/516–516).

TRAIN TRAVEL

Amtrak (☎ 800/872–7245) provides train service in Arizona with bus transfers to Phoenix. Eastbound train passengers will stop in Flagstaff, where Amtrak buses depart daily for Phoenix at 12:45 PM. Westbound train travelers will likely make the transfer in Tucson, where Amtrak-run buses have limited service to Phoenix on Sunday, Tuesday, and Thursday nights at 10:05 PM. The *Sunset Limited* travels three times each week between Los Angeles and Miami, with stops at Yuma, Tucson, and Benson. There is a connecting Amtrak bus (a 2-hour trip) between Tucson and Phoenix. What used to be Phoenix's downtown train terminal is now the **Amtrak Thruway Bus Stop** (✉ 4th Ave. and Harrison St., ☎ 602/253–0121).

TRAVEL AGENCIES

A good travel agent puts your needs first. Look for an agency that has been in business at least five years, emphasizes customer service, and has someone on staff who specializes in your destination. In addition, **make sure the agency belongs to a professional**

trade organization, such as ASTA in the United States. If your travel agency is also acting as your tour operator, *see* Buyer Beware in Tour Operators, *above*).

➤ LOCAL AGENT REFERRALS: **American Society of Travel Agents** (ASTA, ☎ 800/965–2782 24-hr hot line, FAX 703/684–8319). **Association of Canadian Travel Agents** (✉ Suite 201, 1729 Bank St., Ottawa, Ontario K1V 7Z5, ☎ 613/521–0474, FAX 613/521–0805). **Association of British Travel Agents** (✉ 55–57 Newman St., London W1P 4AH, ☎ 0171/637–2444, FAX 0171/637–0713). **Australian Federation of Travel Agents** (☎ 02/9264–3299). **Travel Agents' Association of New Zealand** (☎ 04/499–0104).

U.S. GOVERNMENT

Government agencies can be an excellent source of inexpensive travel information. When planning your trip, **find out what government materials are available.**

➤ PAMPHLETS: **Consumer Information Center** (✉ Consumer Information Catalogue, Pueblo, CO 81009, ☎ 719/948–3334 or 888/878–3256) for a free catalog that includes travel titles.

VISITOR INFORMATION

For general information and brochures contact the Arizona Office of Tourism.

➤ STATEWIDE INFORMATION: **Arizona Office of Tourism** (✉ 2702 N. Third St., Suite 4015, Phoenix 85004, ☎ 602/230–7733 or 888/520–3434, FAX 602/240–5475), open weekdays, 8–5; closed holidays. **Native American Tourism Center** (✉ 4130 N. Goldwater Blvd., Suite 114, ☎ 602/945–0771, FAX 602/945–0264) aids in arranging tourist visits to reservation lands; they can't afford to send information packets, but visitors are welcome to call, fax, or stop in weekdays 8–5. **Phoenix Chamber of Commerce** (✉ Bank One Plaza, 201 N. Central Ave., Suite 2700, Phoenix 85073, ☎ 602/254–5521). **Phoenix and Valley of the Sun Convention and Visitors Bureau** (✉ Arizona Center, 400 E. Van Buren St., Suite 600, Phoenix 85004; ✉ Hyatt Regency Phoenix, 2nd and Adams Sts.; ☎ 602/254–6500 for both). **Scottsdale Chamber of Commerce** (✉ 7343 Scottsdale Mall, Scottsdale 85251, ☎ 602/945–8481 or 800/877–1117) is open weekdays 8:30–6:30, Saturday 10–5, and Sunday 11–5.

WEB SITES

Do **check out the World Wide Web** when you're planning your trip. You'll find everything from up-to-date weather forecasts to virtual tours of famous cities. Fodor's Web site, www.fodors.com, is a great place to start your on-line travels. For more information specifically on Phoenix and Scottsdale, visit the **ARIZONA GUIDE** (www.arizonaguide.com), the official Web site of the Arizona Office of Tourism. Here you'll find video clips of popular destinations, information on everything from golfing hot spots to Indian festivals, and links to related Web sites.

The **Phoenix New Times** (www.phoenixnewtimes.com)

maintains a site with lively features and and insiders' guides to dining, the arts, and nightlife in the Phoenix metro area.

WEATHER

Phoenix averages 300 sunny days and 7 inches of precipitation annually.

PHOENIX

Jan.	67F	18C	May	94F	32C	Sept.	99F	36C
	43	3		66	14		73	20
Feb.	72F	20C	June	103F	37C	Oct.	90F	29C
	46	4		74	19		63	14
Mar.	77F	23C	July	103F	38C	Nov.	74F	23C
	51	7		81	23		49	7
Apr.	85F	28C	Aug.	104F	36C	Dec.	68F	19C
	58	11		79	22		44	4

➤ FORECASTS: The Arizona Republic's **Pressline** (☎ 602/271–5656, then press 1010) gives tomorrow's forecast and up-to-date Valley conditions. **Weatherline** (☎ 602/265–5550) provides three-day forecasts. The **National Weather Service** (☎ 602/379–4000, then press 4) has a local extended forecast recording.

1 Destination: Phoenix and Scottsdale

IN THE VALLEY OF THE SUN

THE EVER-WIDENING Phoenix metropolitan area is a melding of 22 communities and, with a population of more than a million people, the sixth-largest city in the United States. America's fastest-growing urban center provides a tremendous variety of activities—from golfing on championship courses and hiking on some of the country's most popular trails to dining on the ultimate in Southwest cuisine and luxuriating at world-class resorts. Scottsdale and the college town of Tempe are packed with great boutiques and art galleries. Outside of metropolitan Phoenix, Wickenburg is an authentic Old West town, and the Apache Trail drive is one of the most scenic routes in America.

Phoenix and Scottsdale lie in the heart of central Arizona in the Valley of the Sun—named for its 330-plus days of sunshine each year and giving metro Phoenix its nickname, the Valley. This 1,000-square-mi valley is the northern tip of the Sonoran Desert, a rolling expanse of prehistoric seabed that stretches from central Arizona deep into northwestern Mexico. The landscape of the valley can be surprising for those who don't re-

alize just how lush the desert can be. It's studded with cacti, palo verde trees, and creosote bushes, crusted with hard-baked clay and rock, and scorched by summer temperatures that can stay above 100°F for weeks at a time. But its dry skin responds magically to the touch of rainwater. Spring is a miracle of stately saguaro cacti crowned with white flowers, gold and orange poppies, scarlet blossoms bursting from the dry spikes of the ocotillo, hills ablaze with bright yellow creosote, reddish lavender dotting the antlers of the staghorn cholla, and tiny blue flowers clustering on the stems of the desert sage.

The modern-day populating of this desert benefited from centuries of forethought. As the Hohokam people discovered 2,300 years ago, the springtime rains can be augmented by human hands. Having migrated north from northwestern Mexico, they cultivated cotton, corn, and beans in tilled, rowed, and irrigated fields for about 1,700 years, establishing more than 300 mi of canals—an engineering miracle, particularly when you consider the limited technology available. The Hohokam, whose name comes from the Piman word for "people who have gone before," constructed a great town upon whose ruins modern Phoenix is built—and then vanished.

From the time the Hohokam left until the American Civil War, the once fertile Salt River valley lay forgotten, used only by occasional small bands of Pima and Maricopa peoples. Then, in 1865, the U.S. Army established Fort McDowell in the mountains to the east, where the Verde River flows into the Salt. To feed the men and the horses stationed there, Jack Swilling, a former Confederate army officer, had the idea of reopening the Hohokam canals in 1867. Within a year, fields bright with barley and pumpkins earned the area the name of Punkinsville. But by 1870, when the town site was plotted, the 300 inhabitants had decided that their new city would rise "like a phoenix" from the ashes of a vanished civilization.

Phoenix indeed grew steadily. Within 20 years, it had become large enough—at about 3,000 people—to wrest the title of territorial capital from Prescott. By 1912, when Arizona was admitted as a state, the area, irrigated by the brand-new Roosevelt Dam and Salt River Project, had a burgeoning cotton industry. Copper and cattle were mined and raised elsewhere but were banked and traded in Phoenix, and the cattle were slaughtered and packed here in the largest stockyards outside Chicago.

Meanwhile, the climate, so long a crippling liability, became an asset. Desert air was the prescribed therapy for the respiratory ills rampant in the sooty, factory-filled East; Scottsdale began in 1901 as "30-odd tents and a half dozen adobe houses" put up by health seekers. By 1930, visitors looking for warm winter recreation as well as rejuvenating aridity filled the elegant San Marcos Hotel and Arizona Biltmore, first of the many luxury retreats for which the area is now known worldwide.

Phoenix's main growth spurt occurred in the early 1950s when air-conditioning made summers bearable, and the city has experienced the ups and downs of unbridled growth ever since. It's very much a work still in progress; so much is changing, and so quickly, that even long-time residents have a difficult time keeping up. But at the same time, Phoenix and Scottsdale are low-key places where people take things easy and dress informally. If the heat can be a little overwhelming at the height of a summer day, at least it has the salutary effect of slowing the pace of life down to an enjoyable speed. As old desert hands say, you don't begin to see the desert until you've looked at it long enough to see its colors; and you aren't ready to get up and move until you've seen the sun go down.

PLEASURES AND PASTIMES

Baseball

The newly minted Arizona Diamondbacks are the big draw come April, but many fans come in March to watch professional teams warm up for the season in spring-training Cactus League games, most of them in the Phoenix area. The teams start their training camps as much as three weeks earlier. Free drills—held in the morning before an exhibition game—are fun to watch, and there's a good chance you might be able to chat with the players before or after these sessions. In some cases, reserved seats sell out each fall before the upcoming season, but you can almost always get general admission seats on game days.

Dining

Phoenix's culinary traditions arise from a unique blend of Old West and New West cultures. In the mid-19th century, the north-Mexican rancho cooking that had been in Arizona for 150 years was joined by the Anglo-European food of American settlers. Arizona Territory was also an outpost of the West's cattle-ranching boom, and the railroads brought a significant early influx of Chinese settlers.

By the mid-20th century, the Valley was rich in Mexican food, steak houses (Phoenix was a major stockyard center until the 1970s), and Chinese restaurants, mostly Cantonese. Then, during the 1970s, things took off. Southeast Asian refugees introduced spicy Asian dishes that were instantly welcome in a city used to salsa and sweet-and-sour. Immigrants from Central America and the Middle East brought more variations on familiar themes, as well as new approaches. Soon, "southwestern international" was born, and by the late '80s, it had taken hold of America's culinary imagination. Still, Arizona being what it is, Phoenix also has plenty of good old meat-and-potatoes and diner fare.

Golf

Phoenix has become a golf mecca, due to the warm weather, azure skies, and serene vistas of the desert. The explosive growth of the area has brought many new courses to the Valley over the past 15 years, many world-class. The city provides an impressive array of courses—golfers may choose lush, manicured fairways with tranquil lakes and fountains or get right out in the wild dunes and scrub brush of the natural desert.

Hot-Air Ballooning

For a bird's-eye view of the spectacular desert landscape, try a hot-air balloon ride. The peaceful silence of life hundreds of feet up is unforgettable; since the balloon is carried on the wind, you'll experience no wind yourself. In addition to this tranquility, many elusive desert creatures can be viewed in their natural habitats only from a balloon.

Lodging

If there's one thing the Valley of the Sun knows how to do right, it's lodging, and metropolitan Phoenix has options ranging from world-class resorts to roadside motels, from upscale dude ranches to no-frills family-style operations where you can do your own cooking.

Mountains

The Valley of the Sun is ringed by mountains, which provide many options for outdoor activities. Squaw Peak is just north of downtown Phoenix and Camelback Mountain and the Papago Peaks are landmarks between Phoenix and Scottsdale. South of the city, not 5 mi from downtown, rise the much less lofty peaks of South Mountain Park. This 12-mi-wide chain of dry mountains divides the Valley from the rest of the Sonoran Desert.

Shopping

Many tourists come to Arizona for no other reason than to purchase fine Native American jewelry and crafts. Collectibles include Navajo rugs and sand paintings, Hopi kachina dolls (intricately carved and colorful representations of Hopi spiritual beings) and pottery, Tohono O'odham (Papago) basketry, and Apache beadwork, as well as the highly prized silver and turquoise jewelry produced by several different tribes.

FOUR HALF-DAY ITINERARIES

If you're here for just a short period, don't miss the must-see sights. The neighborhood exploring tours in Chapter 2 provide more information about individual sights.

The Cultural Center

Visit the Heard Museum for its acclaimed collection of Native American art and artifacts, and then head south on Central Avenue to browse the artfully designed Phoenix Central Library.

Downtown Interactive Musuems

The interactive exhibits at the Arizona Science Center and Phoenix Museum of History are fun for kids of all ages. Park your car near Heritage Square, which contains the only remaining homes from the original Phoenix townsite. From here it's a short walk to the Phoenix Museum of History, which covers the Anglo development of the area between the 1860s and 1930s. The Arizona Science center is just a couple of blocks to the north and west.

In and Around Scottsdale

Rise early and begin your day with a tour at Frank Lloyd Wright's

Taliesin West, his organically designed wintertime retreat, inspired by the surrounding desert and foothills. Next head back south into Scottsdale for gallery browsing along Main Street or Marshall Way.

For a Cool, Desert Evening

Join the scores of locals hiking after work on the Squaw Peak Summit Trail (☞ Chapter 6). The landmark mountain is a steep 19% grade and stop-off points along the way let you admire the sunset over Phoenix. From this height, the valley resembles a lunar landscape. Instead of a hike, or after it, return south to Papago Park's stunning Desert Botanical Gardens—depending on the season, it's open until 8 or 10 PM. You can see more than 4,000 different species of cacti, succulents, trees, and flowers here.

NEW AND NOTEWORTHY

The 1998 inaugural season of the **Arizona Diamondbacks,** whose owners include actor Billy Crystal, ushered in a new era for baseball in Arizona. Long a popular spot for minor league teams—and major league teams who come for spring training—the state finally has its own National League West team, which plays its home games in stunning Bank One Ballpark in Phoenix. The $345 million facility's 9 million-pound retractable dome makes possible the luxury of real grass (a special variety was developed specifically for the field) and the protection of an indoor park. The Diamondbacks got off to a rough start on the field, but fans have found some consolation at the popular Sun Pool Party Pavilion. The only swimming pool in a major league park, it's just beyond the right-center field wall.

Phoenix's **Heard Museum,** internationally recognized for its exhibits on Native American history, culture, and art, is scheduled to complete its $13.6 million, 50,000-square-ft expansion in March 1999. A new educational facility lies north of the museum's 1929 main building, and a 400-seat auditorium, new galleries, and a café are being added. The museum's archives and library will double in size and be linked by computer to research centers around the world.

2 Exploring Phoenix and Scottsdale

THE SUN BELT BOOM BEGAN when low-cost air-conditioning made summer heat manageable. From 1950 to 1990, the Phoenix urban area more than quadrupled in population, catapulting real estate and home-building into two of the state's biggest industries. Cities—like Scottsdale—planted around Phoenix have become its suburbs, and fields that for decades grew cotton and citrus now grow microchips and homes. Glendale and Peoria on the west side, and Tempe, Mesa, Chandler, and Gilbert on the east, make up the nation's third-largest silicon valley.

Numbers in the text correspond to numbers in the margin and on the Exploring Downtown and the Cultural Center, and Exploring Scottsdale maps.

Downtown Phoenix

The renovated downtown area gives you a look at Phoenix's past and present, as well as a peek at its future. Restored homes from the original townsite give visitors an idea of how far the city has come since its inception around the turn of the last century, while several fine museums point to the Valley of the Sun's increasing sophistication in the coming one.

A Good Walk

Park your car in the parking structure on the southeast corner of 5th and Monroe streets (be prepared, it can be cramped), and begin your tour in the blocks known as the Heritage and Science Park; 5th to 7th streets between Monroe and Adams contain **Heritage Square** ①, the **Arizona Science Center** ②, and the **Phoenix Museum of History** ③. From the corner of 5th and Monroe, walk two blocks west to see **St. Mary's Basilica** ④, Phoenix's first Catholic church. Head north one block to Van Buren Street. On the northeast corner of the intersection, you'll see two glass-clad office towers with a lane of royal palms between them. Follow the palm trees: they lead to the **Arizona Center** ⑤. Leaving the Arizona Center, from the corner of 3rd and Van Buren, walk a block west to 2nd Street and two blocks south on

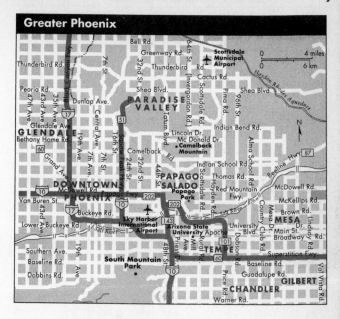

Greater Phoenix

2nd Street, passing the 24-story Hyatt Regency hotel on your right, then another block and a half west on Adams Street to the **Museo Chicano** ⑥. You can walk to Heritage and Science Park from here, catch a DASH shuttle back, or continue on two more blocks west toward the striking facade of the **Orpheum Theatre** ⑦.

If you're really an indefatigable walker, continue south through the plaza on the Orpheum's east side to Washington Street; head east on Washington Street, passing Historic City Hall and the county courthouse on your right. At the intersection of Washington and 1st Avenue, you'll see Patriots Square Park on the southeast corner; cross diagonally (southeast) through the park to the corner of Jefferson Street and Central Avenue. Another block east on Jefferson and then a block south on 1st Street will take you to the site of the **America West Arena** ⑧. From the arena, walk back to Jefferson Street and Central Avenue to catch the DASH shuttle back to your car.

TIMING

In moderate weather, this walk is a pleasant daylong tour; from late May to mid-October, it's best to break it up over two days. Be sure to take advantage of the 35¢ DASH (Downtown Area Shuttle; ☞ Bus Travel *in* Essential Information).

Sights to See

8 America West Arena. This 20,000-seat sports palace is the home of the Phoenix Suns, the Arizona Rattlers arena football team, and the Arizona Sandsharks professional soccer team. Almost a mall in itself—with cafés and shops, in addition to the team offices—it's interesting to tour even when there's no game on. Check out the video art in the lobby, including the three robot figures fashioned out of small televisions. ⊠ *201 E. Jefferson St., at 2nd St.,* ☎ *602/379–2000.*

5 Arizona Center. Beyond an oasis of dramatic fountains and manicured, sunken gardens stands the curved, two-tiered structure that is downtown's most astonishing shopping venue. The first thing you'll see is the Hooter's at the entrance, which in a way sets the tone for the entire mall. More energetically cheesy than truly elegant, the center has souvenir shops (some with nice merchandise), a dozen restaurants spread over two stories, and the state's largest sports bar. There is a variety of chain and specialty stores as well as open-air vendors stationed in the plaza. Love it or hate it, it's impossible to ignore. ⊠ *Van Buren St. between 3rd and 5th Sts.,* ☎ *602/271–4000 or 602/949–4353.*

★ ⓒ **2 Arizona Science Center.** This concrete monolith, designed by Antoine Predock, opened in April 1997. Lively "please touch" exhibits provide an entertaining educational experience for kids and grown-ups alike—learn about the physics of making gigantic soap bubbles and the technology of satellite weather systems, or listen in to the control tower at Sky Harbor airport. Under the dome of Dorrance Planetarium, dazzling computer graphics simulate orbits and eclipses, as well as three-dimensional space flight. The Irene P. Flinn theater has a 50-ft-high projection screen. ⊠ *600 E. Washington St.,* ☎ *602/716–2000.* ☒ *Museum $6.50; combination museum, theater, and planetarium $11.* ⊙ *Daily 10–5.*

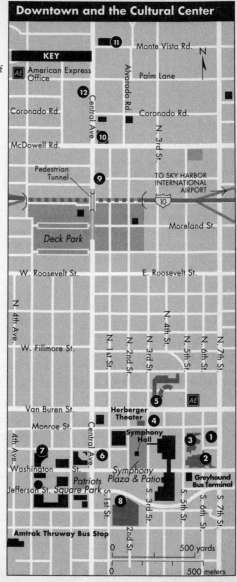

Downtown and the Cultural Center

❶ Heritage Square. In a parklike setting from 5th to 7th streets between Monroe and Adams, this city-owned block contains the only remaining homes from the original Phoenix townsite. On the south side of the square, along Adams Street, stand several houses built between 1899 and 1901. The midwestern-style **Stevens House** holds the **Arizona Doll and Toy Museum** (✉ 602 E. Adams St., ☎ 602/253–9337). Next to it, in the California-style **Stevens-Haustgen House,** is the **Native Ring Project** (✉ 614 E. Adams St., ☎ 602/534–2243), which rotates exhibits from the Pueblo Grande museum collection and sells handcrafted Native American jewelry and gifts. The **Teeter House,** the third house in the row, is a Victorian-style tearoom. The **Silva House** (☎ 602/236–5451), a bungalow from 1900 has presentations about turn-of-the-century life for settlers in the Phoenix township. On the south side of Adams Street, the **Thomas House** and **Baird Machine Shop** are an Italian bakery/pizzeria combination, **Bianco's,** under the hand of the Valley's favorite chef, Chris Bianco.

The queen of Heritage Square is the **Rosson House,** an 1895 gingerbread Victorian in the Queen Anne style. Built by a physician who served a brief term as mayor, it is the sole survivor of the fewer than two dozen Victorians erected in Phoenix. It was bought and restored by the city in 1974. A 30-minute tour of this classic is worth the modest admission price. ✉ *6th and Monroe Sts.,* ☎ *602/262–5071.* ▣ *$3.* ☼ *Wed.–Sat. 10–3:30, Sun. noon–3:30.*

NEED A BREAK?   The Victorian-style tearoom in the **Teeter House** (✉ 622 E. Adams St., ☎ 602/252–4682) serves such authentic tea fare as Devonshire cream, scones with berries, and cucumber sandwiches. Heartier gourmet sandwiches and salads are also available. The staff will box any of your choices, should you prefer to enjoy them on the lawn outside.

❻ Museo Chicano. Artistic works of Hispano-American artists from both the United States and Mexico are showcased here. Exhibits display the broad range of classic and modern Hispanic culture, making this site one of the premier centers for contemporary Latin American art. ✉ *25 E. Adams St.,* ☎ *602/257–5536.* ▣ *$2.* ☼ *Tues.–Sat. 10–4.*

⑦ Orpheum Theatre. The Spanish-colonial–revival architecture and exterior reliefs of this 1929 movie palace have long been admired, and now, after an extensive renovation by artisans and craftspeople, the eclectic ornamental details of the interior have been meticulously restored. Call for details on guided tours or concert schedules. ⊠ *203 W. Adams St.,* ☎ *602/252–9678.*

★ ⌗ **③ Phoenix Museum of History.** This striking glass-and-steel museum, which opened in 1996, offers a healthy dose of regional history from the 1860s (when Anglo settlement began) through the 1930s. A tour through interactive exhibits allows guests to appreciate the city's multicultural heritage as well as witness its growth. Visitors are invited to play Sniff That Barrel (to guess its contents) at a replica of Hancock Store (an 1860s Circle-K equivalent) or take a turn at packing a toy wagon with color-coded blocks as if for a cross-country trip. ⊠ *105 N. 5th St.,* ☎ *602/253–2734.* ⊡ *$5.* ☉ *Mon.–Sat. 10–5, Sun. noon–5.*

④ St. Mary's Basilica. Founded in 1881, Phoenix's first Catholic church presents a stunning facade, its pink stucco and twin towers a pleasant anomaly among the modern concrete of downtown. Inside, the basilica, where Pope John Paul II visited in 1987, has magnificent stained-glass windows designed in Munich. Mass is held daily. ⊠ *Third and Monroe Sts.,* ☎ *602/252–7651.* ⊡ *Free.* ☉ *Hrs vary, call for opening times.*

The Cultural Center

The heart of Phoenix's downtown cultural center is the rolling greensward of the Margaret T. Hance Park, also known as Deck Park. Built atop the I–10 tunnel under Central Avenue, it spreads more than 1 mi from 3rd Avenue on the west to 3rd Street on the east, and ¼ mi from Portland Street north to Culver Street. Completed in 1993, it is the city's second-largest downtown park (the largest is half-century-old Encanto Park, 2 mi northwest). Growing at the same rapid rate as the city itself, this neighborhood has received a giant face-lift as of late—including the construction of a new library and the expansion or renovation of nearly all the area's museums.

A Good Walk

Park free in the lot of the **Phoenix Central Library** ⑨ at the corner of Central Avenue and East Willetta Street. Two blocks north on Central, on the other side of McDowell Road, is the modern, green-stone structure of the **Phoenix Art Museum** ⑩. North of the museum, a slight detour brings a brief respite from the noise and traffic of Central Avenue as well as a glimpse of some lovely residential architecture. Head one block east on Coronado Road to Alvarado Road, then follow Alvarado north for two longish blocks (zigzagging a few feet to the east at Palm Lane) to Monte Vista Road; turn left onto Monte Vista and proceed 50 yards west to the entrance of the **Heard Museum** ⑪. From the Heard, head south on Central Avenue toward the red-granite Viad Tower; its lobby holds the **Breck Girl Hall of Fame** ⑫.

TIMING

You can see all the attractions in one day, but on a hot one it's too much to cover. Bus O runs up and down Central Avenue every 10 minutes on weekdays and every 20 minutes on Saturday.

Sights to See

⑫ **Breck Girl Hall of Fame.** On the ground floor of the red-granite **Viad Corporate Center** is a campy stop sure to be appreciated by pop-culture enthusiasts. This one-room museum contains more than 150 of the signature pastel portraits from the "Breck Girl" shampoo ads—which date from the 1930s—including pictures of Brooke Shields, Kim Basinger, Cybill Shepherd, and other now-famous former Breck Girls. A guide can detail the life and times of Mr. Edward J. Breck, whose lasting contributions to society include being the first person to differentiate between dry and oily. ⊠ *1850 N. Central Ave.,* ☎ *602/207–4000.* 🎟 *Free.* ☉ *Weekdays 11–3.*

| NEED A BREAK? | The grassy park of the **Viad Corporate Center** is a great place to stop for a rest. A string of tiered fountains snakes through the 2-acre park and sculpture garden, which contains lifelike works in bronze—some so realistic, you might unwittingly pass right by them. Stop to appreciate their whimsical touches, such as the blue-capped window washer's paperback copy of *Rear Window* tucked in his overalls. |

★ ☾ ⑪ **Heard Museum.** Pioneer Phoenix settlers Dwight and Maie Heard had a Spanish-colonial–revival building erected on their property to house their impressive collection of southwestern art; today, the site has developed into the nation's premier showcase of Native American art, basketry, pottery, weavings, and bead work—more than 32,000 pieces in all. Children like the interactive art-making exhibits, and events such as the Guild Indian Fair and the Hoop Dancing Competition explore the Native American experience. The museum has the best gift shop in town; it's not cheap, but you can be sure you're getting authentic, high-quality goods. Major expansion is scheduled to be completed in 1999. ⊠ *22 E. Monte Vista Rd.,* ☎ *602/252–8848 or 602/ 252–8840.* ☜ *$6.* ☉ *Mon.–Sat. 9:30–5, Sun. noon–5.*

⑩ **Phoenix Art Museum.** The green quartz exterior of this modern museum adds yet another piece of eye-catching architecture to Central Avenue. More than 13,000 objets d'art are on display inside, including 18th- and 19th-century European works and the American West collection, which features painters from Frederic Remington to Georgia O'Keeffe. A clothing-and-costume collection has pieces from 1750, and the Asian art gallery is filled with fine Chinese porcelain and pieces of intricate cloisonné. ⊠ *1625 N. Central Ave.,* ☎ *602/257–1222 or 602/257–1800.* ☜ *$4; tours free.* ☉ *Tues. and Thurs.–Sat. 10–5, Wed. 10– 9, Sun. noon–5.*

⑨ **Phoenix Central Library.** Architect Will Bruder's magnificent 1995 contribution to Central Avenue is absolutely worth a stop. The curved building's copper-penny exterior evokes images of the region's sunburnt mesas; inside, skylights, glass walls, and computer-controlled mirrors keep the structure bathed in natural light. A five-story glass atrium, known as the Crystal Canyon, is best appreciated from a speedy ride in one of three glass elevators. At the top, from the largest reading room in North America, check out a cable-suspended steel ceiling that appears to float overhead. Free one-hour tours are offered on Fridays; call to arrange in advance. ⊠ *1221 N. Central Ave.,* ☎ *602/262–4636; 602/262–6582 tour reservations.* ☉ *Mon.–Wed. 9–9, Thurs.–Sat. 9–6, Sun. 1–5.*

NEED A
BREAK?

Willow House (⊠ 149 W. McDowell Rd., ☎ 602/252–0272) is the area's most comfortable coffeehouse in a funky, friendly environment. Grab a sandwich, dessert, or coffee and stretch out in a low-slung couch underneath brightly painted walls. Artwork is on display, and kaleidoscopic fish swim along the rest-room walls.

South Phoenix

A mostly residential area and home to much of Phoenix's substantial Hispanic population, South Phoenix is worth a visit for two reasons: its family-style restaurants and roadside stands offer some of the best Mexican food in the city, and it's home to South Mountain Park and the Mystery Castle, two of Phoenix's most remarkable sights.

Sights to See

★ **Mystery Castle.** At the foot of South Mountain lies a curious dwelling fashioned from desert rocks, railroad refuse, and anything else its builder, Boyce Gulley, could get his hands on. Boyce's daughter Mary Lou lives here now and leads tours. Full of fascinating oddities, the castle has 18 rooms with 13 fireplaces, 90 bottle-glass portholes, a downstairs grotto tavern, and a roll-away bed with a mining railcar as its frame. Check out the pipe organ of Elsie, the Widow of Tombstone, who buried six husbands under rather suspicious circumstances. ⊠ *800 E. Mineral Rd., at the end of S. 7th St.,* ☎ *602/268–1581.* ☞ *$4.* ☉ *Tues.–Sun. 11–4.*

★ **South Mountain Park.** This desert wonderland, the world's largest city park (almost 17,000 acres), offers an outdoor experience unparalleled in the Valley: a wilderness of mountain/desert trails (☞ Hiking in Chapter 6) for hikers, bikers, and horseback riders. Roads climb past buildings constructed during the New Deal era, winding through desert flora to the trailheads; scenic overlooks reveal the distant Phoenix skyline, which seems a world away from this wild and luxuriant oasis. Look for ancient petroglyphs (rock engravings, often of animals or flora); try to spot a desert cottontail rabbit or chuckwalla lizard; or simply stroll among the wondrous flora. It's an electrifying experience, all the more startling for being placed right on the edge of a major metropolis. ⊠ *10919 S. Central Ave.,* ☎ *602/495–5078.*

TIMING

Depending on how long you spend in the park, this tour can be done in a couple of hours or can stretch to an entire day. Leave about a half hour each way for driving, an hour to an hour and a half at the castle, and anywhere from a 20-minute drive to an all-day hike in South Mountain.

Papago Salado

The word "Papago," meaning "bean eater," was a term given by 16th-century Spanish explorers to a vanished native people of the Phoenix area. Farmers of the desert, the Hohokam (as they are more properly called) grew corn, beans, squash, and cotton. They lived in central Arizona from about AD 1 to 1450, at which point their civilization collapsed and disappeared for reasons unknown—some conjecture drought, floods, or internal strife—abandoning the Salt River (Rio Salado) valley but leaving behind remains of villages and a complex system of irrigation canals. The Papago Salado region is located between Phoenix and Tempe and contains the Pueblo Grande ruins, the Desert Botanical Garden, the Phoenix Zoo, and a variety of potential recreational activities amid the buttes of Papago Park.

A GOOD DRIVE

Stop at the **Pueblo Grande Museum and Cultural Park,** on Washington Street between 44th Street and the Hohokam Expressway (AZ 143). Follow Washington Street east 3½ mi to Priest Drive and turn north. Priest Drive becomes Galvin Parkway north of Van Buren Street; follow signs to entrances for the **Phoenix Zoo** and **Papago Park,** or to the **Desert Botanical Garden.** To visit the **Hall of Flame** afterward, drive south on Galvin Parkway to Van Buren Street; turn east on Van Buren and drive ⅛ mi, turning south at Project Drive (at the buff-color stone marker that reads SALT RIVER PROJECT).

TIMING

Seeing all the sights requires the better part of a day. You may want to save the Desert Botanical Garden for the end of your tour, as it stays open until 8 PM October–April and

10 PM May–September and is particularly lovely when lit by the setting sun or by moonlight.

Sights to See

★ ℭ **Desert Botanical Garden.** Opened in 1939 to conserve and showcase the ecology of the desert, these 150 acres contain more than 4,000 different species of cacti, succulents, trees, and flowers. A stroll along the ½-mi-long "Plants and People of the Sonoran Desert" trail is a fascinating lesson in environmental adaptations; children will enjoy playing the self-guiding game "Desert Detective." ⊠ *1201 N. Galvin Pkwy.,* ☎ *602/941–1217 or 602/941–1225.* ✑ *$7.* ☉ *Oct.–Apr., daily 8–8; May–Sept., daily 7 AM–10 PM.*

NEED A BREAK?	If you're headed to this area from downtown Phoenix, stop in **Kohnie's Coffee** (⊠ 4225 E. Camelback Rd. ☎ 602/952-9948) for coffee, pastries, bagels, and scones. It's open at 6:30 AM (8 AM Sunday) and closed by 2 PM (noon on weekends).

ℭ **Hall of Flame.** Retired firefighters lead tours through more than 100 restored fire engines and tell harrowing tales of the "world's most dangerous profession." Kids can climb on a 1916 engine, operate alarm systems, and learn lessons of fire safety from the pros. More than 3,000 helmets, badges, and other fire-fighting-related articles are on display, dating from as far back as 1725. ⊠ *6101 E. Van Buren St.,* ☎ *602/275–3473.* ✑ *$4.* ☉ *Mon.–Sat. 9–5, Sun. noon–4; tours at 2.*

Papago Park. A blend of hilly desert terrain, streams, and lagoons, this park has picnic areas, a Frisbee-golf course, a playground, hiking and biking trails, and even large-mouth bass and trout fishing (urban fishing license required for anglers age 15 and over—pick one up at sporting-goods or Circle-K stores). The hike up to landmark **Hole-in-the-Rock** is popular—but remember that it's much easier to climb up to the hole than to get down. **Governor Hunt's Tomb,** the white pyramid at the top of ramada 16, commemorates the former Arizona leader and provides a lovely view. ⊠ *625 N. Galvin Pkwy.,* ☎ *602/256–3220.* ☉ *Daily 6 AM–midnight.*

🐾 **Phoenix Zoo.** Five designated trails wind through this 125-acre zoo, which has replicas of such habitats as an African savanna and a tropical rain forest. Meerkats, warthogs, desert bighorn sheep, and endangered Arabian oryx are among the unusual sights, as is Ruby the artistic Asian elephant and Uco, the endangered spectacled bear from South America. The Children's Trail introduces small mammals, and a stop at the big red barn provides a chance to help groom goats and sheep. The 30-minute narrated safari train tour costs $2 and provides a good overview of the park. In December, the popular "Zoo Lights" exhibit transforms the area into an enchanted forest of more than 600,000 twinkling lights, many in the shape of the zoo's residents. ⊠ *455 N. Galvin Pkwy.,* ☎ *602/273–7771.* 🎫 *$8.50.* ☉ *Daily 9–5; call for special summer hrs May–Labor Day.*

★ **Pueblo Grande Museum and Cultural Park.** Phoenix's only national landmark, this park was once the site of a 500-acre Hohokam village supporting about 1,000 people and containing homes, storage rooms, cemeteries, and several ball courts. Three exhibition galleries hold displays on the Hohokam culture, archaeological methods, and other Southwest themes; kids will like the hands-on, interactive learning center. View the 10-minute orientation video before heading out on the ½-mi Ruin Trail past excavated mounds and ruined structures that give a hint of the Hohokams' savvy: there's a building whose corner doorway was perfectly placed to watch the summer solstice sunrise and winter solstice sunset. ⊠ *4619 E. Washington St.,* ☎ *602/495–0901.* 🎫 *$2; free Sun.* ☉ *Mon.–Sat. 9–4:45, Sun. 1–4:45.*

Scottsdale

Historic sites, nationally known art galleries, and souvenir shops fill downtown Scottsdale; a quick walking tour can easily turn into an all-day excursion if you browse. Historic Old Town Scottsdale features the look of the Old West, while 5th Avenue is known for shopping and Native American jewelry and crafts stores. Cross onto Main Street and enter a world frequented by the international art set (Scottsdale has the third-largest artist community in the United States); discover more galleries and interior-design shops along Marshall Way.

A Good Walk

Park in the free public lot on the corner of 2nd Street and Wells Fargo Avenue, east of Scottsdale Road. A portion of the garage has a three-hour limit; go to upper levels that don't carry time restrictions, as enforcement is strict.

Start your walk by exiting the parking structure from its northeast corner, where a short brick-paved sidewalk leads northward to the plaza of Scottsdale Mall. You'll immediately come upon the **Scottsdale Center for the Arts** ⑬. Stroll counterclockwise around the Mall's lovely grounds, passing Scottsdale's library and municipal buildings, and ending up on the plaza's west side by the **Scottsdale Chamber of Commerce** ⑭ and **Scottsdale Historical Museum** ⑮. Continue west to the intersection of Brown Avenue and Main Street to reach the heart of **Old Town Scottsdale** ⑯, occupying four square blocks from Brown Avenue to Scottsdale Road, between Indian School Road and 2nd Street. From Main Street in Old Town, cross Scottsdale Road to the central drag of the **Main Street Arts District** ⑰. Turn north onto Goldwater Boulevard and gallery-stroll for another two blocks. At Indian School Road, head one block east to the **Marshall Way Arts District** ⑱. Continue two blocks north on Marshall Way to the fountain of prancing Arabian horses that marks **Fifth Avenue** ⑲. You can catch the trolley back to Scottsdale Mall here, on the south side of the intersection of 5th Avenue and Stetson Drive, or walk the five blocks south on Scottsdale Road and one block east on Main Street.

Not far from downtown Scottsdale are three other worthy attractions: the **Buffalo Museum, Taliesin West** (Frank Lloyd Wright's winter home), and the lovely **Fleischer Museum.**

TIMING

Plan to spend a full day in Scottsdale, as there's a lot to take in between the countless galleries and shops. Although your tour can easily be completed on foot, a trolley runs through the downtown area and out to several resorts: Ollie the Trolley charges $5 for an all-day pass, though service in downtown Scottsdale is free (☎ 602/970–8130 for information). Also look for horse-drawn Arizona Carriage

Company (☎ 602/423–1449), whose Cinderella-like carriages provide romantic transportation throughout Old Town Scottsdale ($20 for 15-minute tours, $40 for ½ hour, $70 for an hour for carriages that hold up to six). They're also perfect props for snapshots.

If you're interested in touring the galleries, visit on a Thursday and do the Scottsdale **Art Walk** (☎ 602/990–3939), held from 7 to 9 PM each Thursday year-round (except Thanksgiving). Main Street and Marshall Way, the two major gallery strips, take on a party atmosphere during the evening hours when tourists *and* locals are browsing: the Scottsdale community supports local arts.

Sights to See

Buffalo Museum of America. Tucked away in a Scottsdale shopping plaza, this eclectic little museum pays homage to the American bison, or buffalo, and its important role in American history. The museum's contents range from the awesome shaggy beast itself—courtesy of modern taxidermy—to a variety of original commissioned works of fine art, to props from the film "Dances with Wolves." The "Buffalo Bill Room" showcases the legendary hunter's personal possessions, and the downstairs gift shop is a mélange of all things buffalo—clocks, banks, tins, plates, old stereoscope cards, even a promotional poster from Hunter S. Thompson's novel *Where The Buffalo Roam.* ⊠ 10261 N. Scottsdale Rd., ☎ 602/951–1022. ☞ $3. ⊙ Weekdays 9–5.

⑲ Fifth Avenue. For more than 40 years, this shopping stretch has been home to a collection of boutiques and specialty shops. Whether you're seeking handmade Native American arts and crafts, casual clothing, or cacti, you'll find it here—plus colorful storefronts, friendly merchants, even an old "cigar store" Indian. After a full day of paintings, turquoise jewelry, and knickknacks, children especially may enjoy casting their eyes upon the six-story monster screen of the **IMAX Theater** (⊠ 4343 N. Scottsdale Rd., ☎ 602/945–4629), at the east end of the avenue. ⊠ *5th Ave. between Goldwater Blvd. and Scottsdale Rd.*

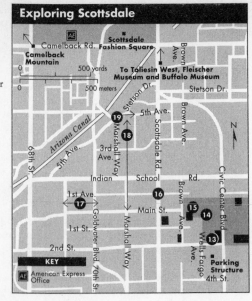

Exploring Scottsdale

Fleischer Museum. Housed in the corporate Perimeter Center, this collection is an undiscovered gem. More than 80 artists from the California School of Impressionism, which is noted for its brightly colored plein air painting, are represented, including such notables as William Wendt and Franz A. Bischoff. It's worth a trip to the somewhat out-of-the-way location. ⊠ *17207 N. Perimeter Dr., at the intersection of Pima and Bell Rds.,* ☎ *602/585–3108.* ⌨ *Free.* ☉ *Daily 10–4. Closed holidays.*

★ ⓘ **Main Street Arts District.** Gallery after gallery on Main Street and First Avenue, particularly on the blocks between Scottsdale Road and 69th Street, displays artwork of myriad styles—contemporary, western realism, Native American, and traditional. Several antiques shops are also here; specialties include elegant porcelains and china, fine antique jewelry, and Oriental rugs.

NEED A
BREAK? For a light meal during daytime gallery-hopping, try **Arcadia Farms** (✉ 7014 E. 1st Ave., ☎ 602/941-5665), where such eclectic fare as raspberry–goat cheese salad and rose-mary-seasoned focaccia with chicken, roasted eggplant, and feta cheese are prepared lovingly. Enjoy a cool drink or a justly popular lemon roulade pastry on the brick patio shaded by African sumac trees.

⑱ Marshall Way Arts District. Another niche of galleries that exhibit mostly contemporary art lines the blocks of Marshall Way north of Indian School Road. Upscale gift and jewelry stores can be found here too. Farther north on Marshall Way across 3rd Avenue, the street is filled with more art galleries and creative stores with a southwestern flair.

⑯ Old Town Scottsdale. Billed as "the West's Most Western Town," this area of Scottsdale features rustic storefronts and wooden sidewalks; it's touristy, but it also gives visitors a genuine taste of life here 80 years ago. You'll find high-quality jewelry, pots, and Mexican imports along with the expected kitschy souvenirs.

⑬ Scottsdale Center for the Arts. Galleries within this cultural and entertainment complex rotate exhibits frequently, with an emphasis on contemporary art and artists. The airy and bright **Museum Store** (☎ 602/874-4464) has a great collection of unusual jewelry, as well as stationery, posters, and art books. ✉ 7380 E. 2nd St., ☎ 602/994-2787. ➡ *Free.* ☉ *Mon.–Sat. 10–5, Thurs. 10–8, Sun. noon–5; also open during performance intermissions.*

⑭ Scottsdale Chamber of Commerce. Pop inside to pick from local maps, guidebooks, and brochures. Ask for a walking-tour map of Old Town Scottsdale's historic sites, which the helpful staff will be pleased to provide. ✉ *7343 Scottsdale Mall,* ☎ *602/945-8481 or 800/877-1117.* ☉ *Weekdays 8:30–6:30, Sat. 10–5, Sun. 11–5.*

⑮ Scottsdale Historical Museum. Scottsdale's first schoolhouse, this redbrick building houses a version of the 1910 schoolroom, as well as photographs, original furniture from the city's founding fathers, and displays of other treasures from Scottsdale's early days. ✉ *7333 Scottsdale Mall,*

☎ 602/945–4499. 🖃 *Free.* ⊘ *Wed.–Sat. 10–5, Sun. noon–5. Closed July–Aug. and holidays.*

OFF THE
BEATEN
PATH

TALIESIN WEST – Ten years after visiting Arizona in 1927 to consult on designs for the Biltmore hotel, architect Frank Lloyd Wright chose 600 acres of raw, rugged Sonoran Desert at the foothills of the McDowell Mountains, just outside Scottsdale, as the site for his permanent winter residence. Wright and apprentices constructed a "desert camp" here, using "organic architecture" to integrate the buildings with respect for the natural setting of the land. An ingenious harmony of indoor and outdoor space is the result; in addition to the living quarters, drafting studio, and small apartments of the Apprentice Court, Taliesin West also has two theaters, a music pavilion, and the "Sun Trap"—a charming structure of sleeping spaces surrounding an open patio and fireplace. Two guided tours cover different parts of the interior, and a guided "Desert Walk" winds through the petroglyphs and landscape, as well as the experimental desert residences designed by his apprentices. Tour times vary, so call ahead; all visitors must be accompanied by a guide. ✉ *12621 Frank Lloyd Wright Blvd.,* ☎ *602/860–8810 or 602/860–2700.* 🖃 *Guided tour (1 hr) $10 winter, $8 summer; Behind the Scenes tour (3 hrs) $25 winter, $20 summer; Desert Walk tour (90 mins) $12.* ⊘ *Daily 8:30–5:30, winter; 7:30–4:30, summer.*

Tempe

Charles Trumbell Hayden arrived on the east end of the Salt River in the 1860s. There he built a flour mill and began a ferry service to cross the then-flowing Rio Salado (Salt River), founding the town then known as Hayden's Ferry in 1871. Other settlers soon arrived, including an Englishman who felt—upon approaching the town from Phoenix and seeing the butte, river, and fields of green mesquite—that the name should be changed to Tempe after the Vale of Tempe in Greek mythology. Hayden took umbrage at the suggested name change but finally relented in 1879.

Today Tempe is Arizona's sixth-largest city and the home of Arizona State University's main campus and a thriving student population. A 20- to 30-minute drive from Phoenix, the tree- and brick-lined Mill Avenue (on which Hayden's mill still stands) is the main drag, rife with student-oriented hangouts, bookstores, boutiques, eateries, and a repertory movie house.

Tempe's banks of the now-dry Rio Salado are the future site of a sprawling commercial and entertainment district, which includes plans to refill the river using inflatable dams and ply the waters once again with ferry service.

A Good Walk

Parking is available in the public structure at Hayden Square, just north of 5th Street and west of Mill Avenue. Begin at **La Casa Vieja,** on the southwest corner of Mill Avenue and 1st Street, to view the restaurant's historical photographs of Tempe. Head south on Mill Avenue toward the main part of town, passing the old Hayden flour mill, as well as "A" Mountain to your left. Continue south along shop-lined Mill Avenue until you reach 5th Street; walk a block east on 5th toward the inverted pyramid of **Tempe City Hall.** Follow the pathway west through the grounds of City Hall and Plazita de Descanso, back to Mill Avenue. Head two blocks south on Mill to University Drive; proceed to Gammage Parkway, where you'll find the Grady Gammage Auditorium and ASU art museums and galleries on the southwest corner of the **Arizona State University** campus. You can walk back up Mill Avenue, catch the free FLASH shuttle northward (it stops on the north corner of Gammage Parkway and Mill Avenue), or wind your way northward through the university campus up toward Sun Devil Stadium.

TIMING

If you're planning to shop as well as tour the campus and museums, allow four or five hours for exploring (and taking periodic breaks) in downtown Tempe.

Sights to See

Arizona State University. What was formerly the Tempe Normal School for Teachers—in 1886, a four-room redbrick building and 20-acre cow pasture—is now the sprawling 750-

acre campus of ASU, home to the largest student population in the Southwest. Stop by the **ASU Visitor Information Center** (⊠ 826 E. Apache Blvd., at Rural Rd., ☎ 602/965–0100) for a copy of a self-guided walking tour (it's a long walk from Mill Avenue, so you might opt for the short tour below). You'll wind past public art and innovative architecture—including a music building that bears a strong resemblance to a wedding cake (designed by Taliesin students to echo Wright's Gammage Auditorium) and a law library shaped like an open book—and end up at the 74,000-seat **ASU Sun Devil Stadium,** home to the school's Sun Devils, headquarters for the NFL's Arizona Cardinals, and the site of Super Bowl XXX.

Heralded for its superior acoustics, the circular **Grady Gammage Auditorium** (⊠ Mill Ave. at Apache Blvd., ☎ 602/965–4050) was the last public structure completed by architect Frank Lloyd Wright, who detached the rear wall from grand tier and balcony sections in an effort to surround every patron with sound. The stage can accommodate a full symphony orchestra, as well as a 2,909-pipe organ. Artwork is exhibited in the lobby and in two on-site galleries, and free half-hour tours are offered weekdays 1–3:30 during the regular school year.

While touring the west end of the campus, stop into the gray-purple stucco **Nelson Fine Arts Center** (☎ 602/965–2787), just north of the Gammage Auditorium. The center's museum houses some fine examples of 19th- and 20th-century painting and sculpture by masters such as Winslow Homer, Edward Hopper, Georgia O'Keeffe, and Rockwell Kent; it's a surprisingly extensive collection for a small museum. You'll also find works by faculty and student artists and an interesting gift shop. 🎨 *Free.* ☉ *Tues. 10–9, Wed.–Sat. 10–5, Sun. 1–5.*

A short walk east, just north of the Hayden Library, ASU's experimental gallery and collection of crockery and ceramics are located in the **Matthews Center** (☎ 602/965–2875). ☉ *Tues.–Sat. 10–5. Closed in summer.*

In Matthews Hall, the **Northlight Gallery** (☎ 602/965–6517) exhibits works by both renowned and emerging photographers. Admission to all ASU museums is free. ☉ *Mon.–Thurs. 10:30–4:30, Sun. noon–4:30.*

La Casa Vieja. In 1871, when Tempe was still known as Hayden's Ferry, this "old house" was built as the home of founding father Charles Hayden. The adobe hacienda is modeled after Spanish mansions and was the town's first building. The late Carl Hayden, former U.S. senator from Arizona, was born here. Now a steak house, the lobby and dining rooms contain photographs and historical documents pertaining to the frontier history of the hamlet of Tempe. ⊠ *3 W. 1st St.,* ☎ *602/967–7594.* ☉ *Sun.–Thurs. 11–11, Fri.– Sat. 11 AM–midnight.*

Tempe City Hall. Local architects Rolf Osland and Michael Goodwin constructed this inverted pyramid not just to win design awards (which they have) but also to shield city workers from the desert sun. The pyramid is constructed mainly of bronzed glass and stainless steel; the point is conceptually buried in a sunken courtyard lushly landscaped with jacaranda, ivy, and flowers, out of which the pyramid widens to the sky: stand underneath and gaze up for a weird fish-eye perspective. ⊠ *31 E. 5th St., 1 block east of Mill Ave.,* ☎ *602/967–2001.* ⊠ *Free.*

NEED A BREAK? The outdoor patio of the **Coffee Plantation** (⊠ 680 S. Mill Ave., ☎ 602/829–7878) is a lively social scene—students cramming, local residents chatting, and poets and musicians presenting their latest works. For a fuller meal, check out **Caffe Boa** (⊠ 709 S. Mill Ave., ☎ 602/968–9112). This friendly spot offers outdoor as well as indoor dining; the upbeat young staff will serve you a variety of creations, from *panini* and *crostini* to such specials as butternut squash soup, seafood ravioli, and grilled prawns in Thai pesto.

3 Dining

ONCE A SLEEPY BACKWATER, the ever-growing Phoenix, Scottsdale, and their environs draw millions of visitors every year: tourists, conventioneers, and winter snowbirds who roost for months at a time. The population boom has been matched by an astonishing restaurant renaissance. Inventive local chefs have put southwestern cuisine on the world culinary map, and the native dishes of the area's newer ethnic communities—Persian, Ethiopian, Salvadoran, Vietnamese—have added another dimension to the local palate. Authentic Thai, Chinese, and Indian restaurants are thriving, and there's superb south-of-the-border food from every region of Mexico. Travelers with sophisticated tastes will be thrilled with the area's restaurants, some ranked among the country's best.

By Howard Seftel

Restaurants are remarkably casual. Except for a handful of high-end spots, slacks and sports shirt are dressy enough for men; pants or a simple skirt are appropriate for women.

Remember that restaurants change hours, locations, chefs, prices, and menus frequently, so it's best to call ahead to confirm. Show up without notice during tourist season, and you may find the drive-through window the only place in town without a two-hour wait. All listed restaurants serve dinner and are open for lunch unless otherwise specified.

CATEGORY	COST*
$$$$	over $35
$$$	$25–$35
$$	$15–$25
$	under $15

*per person for a three-course dinner, excluding drinks, service, and sales tax (6%–7%)

Scottsdale

American

$$$–
$$$$
✕ **The Grill at the TPC.** Everything is way over par at The Grill: this clubhouse grill is one of the best restaurants in town, but it's not for thrill-seeking foodies after great adventures in modern gastronomy. It is the place for prime

steaks, both dry-aged and wet-aged beef, and stunning seafood, flown in fresh daily. For proof, try the house-smoked shark or phenomenal peppercorn-crusted ahi tuna. The ultrarich banana cream pie, spiked with shards of white and dark chocolate, restores this much-abused sweet to its former glory. ⊠ *7575 E. Princess Dr. (Scottsdale Princess resort)*, ☎ *602/585–4848. AE, D, DC, MC, V.*

$$$– $$$$ ★   ✕ **Rancho Pinot Grill.** The attention to quality paid by the husband-and-wife proprietors here—he manages, she cooks—has made this one of the town's top eating spots. The inventive menu changes daily, depending on what's fresh. If you're lucky, you might come on a day when the kitchen features *posole,* a mouthwatering broth with hominy, salt pork, and cabbage. Entrées include quail with soba noodles, rosemary-infused chicken with Italian sausage, and grilled sea bass atop basmati rice. ⊠ *6208 N. Scottsdale Rd.,* ☎ *602/468–9463. Reservations essential. AE, D, MC, V. Closed Sun. and Mon. and mid-Aug.–mid-Sept. No lunch.*

$$$ ✕ **Cowboy Ciao.** Looking for a culinary kick? This kitchen weds southwestern fare and Italian flair, and it's no shotgun wedding, either. The chef delicately sears carpaccio (thin-sliced beef) then coats it with pepper, drizzles it with chili oil, and tops it with shavings of pecorino Romano. Main dishes like Chianti-marinated filet mignon, fennel-seasoned meat loaf, and wild mushrooms in an ancho chili cream sauce heaped over polenta are creative without going off the deep end. The chocolate lottery—complete with an actual lottery ticket—is a dessert hoot. The imaginative wine list has affordable flights that let you taste several wines with your meal. ⊠ *7133 E. Stetson,* ☎ *602/948–3111. AE, D, DC, MC, V. No lunch.*

$$$ ✕ **Don & Charlie's.** A favorite with major-leaguers in town for spring training, this venerable chophouse specializes in prime-grade steak and baseball memorabilia—the walls are covered with pictures, autographs, and uniforms. The New York sirloin, prime rib, and double-thick lamb chops are a hit; sides include au gratin potatoes and creamed spinach. Serious carnivores will not strike out here. ⊠ *7501 E. Camelback Rd.,* ☎ *602/990–0900. AE, D, DC, MC, V. No lunch.*

$$$ ✕ **Gregory's Grill.** This charming bistro is tiny, with seating for maybe 20 patrons. The menu is equally small, but outstanding. Look for appetizers like duck prosciutto, salmon seviche, and a lovely tower fashioned from veggies and goat cheese. Entrées include beer-marinated beef tenderloin, apple-crusted salmon, and grilled pork chops with quinoa risotto. Note: You can save a bundle by bringing your own beer or wine. ⊠ 7049 E. McDowell Rd. (Papago Plaza shopping center), ☎ 602/946–8700. AE, D, MC, V. Closed Sun. No lunch.

$$$ ✕ **Michael's at the Citadel.** One of this town's best-looking places (check out the brick-lined waterfall at the entrance), Michael's contemporary American fare is as elegant as the setting. The entrées are the real stars here: pan-seared duck paired with foie gras and pearl couscous; sesame-crusted swordfish with green coconut curry; venison with a dried-cherry demiglaze; grilled lamb with a goat-cheese potato tart. If you're celebrating a special occasion, Michael's is the spot. ⊠ 8700 E. Pinnacle Peak Rd., ☎ 602/515–2575. AE, D, DC, MC, V. No lunch.

$$$ ✕ **Roaring Fork.** The restaurant's name is supposed to reflect what the chef calls "Western American cuisine." It means appetizers like the cornmeal crepe, stuffed with portobello mushrooms and coated in red pepper sauce, or the smashing cracked-corn stuffing, teamed with turkey confit and dried figs. Two particularly outstanding entrées are skillet-seared pompano, embellished with crawfish and smoked ham hock, and riveting sugar-and-chili-cured duck, served with green chili macaroni. The dessert highlight is the tarte Tatin, here made with pears, not the apples, and goosed up with a vigorous ginger snap. ⊠ 7243 E. Camelback Rd., ☎ 602/947–0795, AE, D, DC, MC, V. Closed Sun. No lunch Sat.

$–$$ ✕ **Bandera.** If you're looking for a quick, tasty dinner before a night out on the town, try this casual, high-volume spot. The weekly menu includes wonderfully moist and meaty rotisserie chicken; you'll see the birds spinning in the big window before you even walk through the door. If you're not a poultry fan, salads, fresh fish, prime rib, and meat loaf usually make it on the menu. The mashed potatoes are divine—you'll think mom is in the kitchen peeling spuds. If you get here at prime eating hours, especially on weekends, be prepared to wait for a table. ⊠ 3821 N. Scottsdale Rd., ☎ 602/994–3524. Reservations not accepted. AE, MC, V. No lunch.

32

Phoenix and Scottsdale Dining

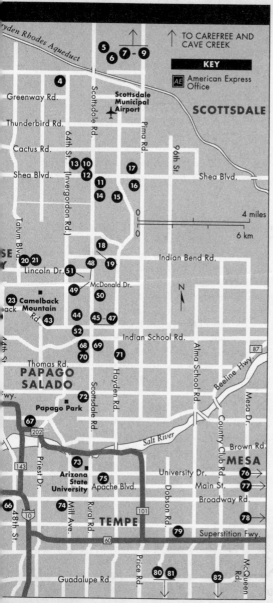

Hayden Rhodes Aqueduct

TO CAREFREE AND
CAVE CREEK

SCOTTSDALE

KEY

AE American Express
Office

Greenway Rd.

Scottsdale Municipal
Airport

Thunderbird Rd.

Cactus Rd.

Shea Blvd.

Shea Blvd.

64th St. (Invergordon Rd.)

Scottsdale Rd.

Pima Rd.

90th St.

0   4 miles

0   6 km

Indian Bend Rd.

Lincoln Dr.

McDonald Dr.

N

Camelback
Mountain

Rd.

Indian School Rd.

Beeline Hwy.

87

Alma School Rd.

Country Club Rd.

Mesa Dr.

Thomas Rd.

**PAPAGO
SALADO**

Hayden Rd.

Scottsdale Rd.

Papago Park

Salt River

Brown Rd.

MESA

202

143

Priest Dr.

**Arizona
State
University**

Apache Blvd.

University Dr.

Main St.

Broadway Rd.

76

77

67

73

75

66

48th St.

10

Mill Ave.

Rural Rd.

101

TEMPE

Dobson Rd.

60

Superstition Fwy.

78

79

Guadalupe Rd.

Price Rd.

McQueen Rd.

80 81

82

$–$$ ✕ **Pinnacle Peak Patio.** This spot is strictly for tourists, but it's no trap. More than 1,600 diners can sit inside this western restaurant, the largest in the world; another 1,400 can dine under the stars out on the patio. Founded in 1957, the Peak hasn't altered its menu in years—a menu that consists solely of five grilled steaks and hickory-roasted chicken. "Big Marv" Dickson has personally manned the grill since 1961, cooking up more than 2 million pounds of beef himself—he credits delectable porterhouse and T-bones to mesquite smoke's magic, but everyone else knows Marv as a Steak Jedi, with a sixth sense for beef. Country bands play nightly. Wear a tie you don't mind leaving behind. ⊠ 10426 E. Jomax Rd., Scottsdale, ☎ 602/967–8082. AE, D, DC, MC, V. No lunch Mon.–Sat.

Asian

$$$ ✕ **Restaurant Hapa.** "Hapa" is Hawaiian slang for "half,"
★ which describes the half-Japanese, half-American background of the chef. But there's nothing halfway about Hapa's astonishingly flavorful, Asian-inspired cuisine. Appetizers like skillet-roasted mussels coated in a Thai-inspired broth scented with lemongrass, mint, basil, ginger, and coconut let you know you're in for a big-time experience. The signature entrée is beef tenderloin, lined with hot Chinese mustard and caramelized brown sugar. Desserts are just as inspired as the other courses: look for the Asian pear cake with lemongrass ice cream, or the coconut crème brûlée tart. ⊠ 6204 N. Scottsdale Rd., ☎ 602/998–8220. MC, V. Closed Sun. No lunch Sat.

$$$ ✕ **Roy's.** Roy Yamaguchi, a James Beard award-winning chef and one of the pioneers of Pacific Rim cooking, has 13 restaurants scattered all over the globe. Look for inventive dishes like steamed pork and crab buns with a spicy Maui onion–black bean sauce; lemongrass tempura chicken breast; tiger prawns on a lobster Alfredo sauce; and nori-crusted ono with a hot and sour red pepper sauce. It's sophisticated food for sophisticated palates. ⊠ 7001 N. Scottsdale Rd. (Scottsdale Seville), ☎ 602/905–1155. AE, MC, V. Closed Sun. No lunch Sat.

$$–$$$ ✕ **Sushi on Shea.** You may be in the middle of the desert, but the Sushi here will make you think you're at the ocean's edge. Yellowtail, toro, shrimp, scallops, freshwater eel, and even monkfish liver pâté are among the long list of delights here. Check out the *nabemono* (hot pot or meals-in-a-bowl) prepared at your table. The best dish? Maybe it's the *una-ju* (broiled freshwater eel with a sublime smoky scent), served over sweet rice. The fact that some people believe eel is an aphrodisiac only adds to its charms. ✉ *7000 E. Shea Blvd.,* ☎ *602/483–7799. AE, D, DC, MC, V. No lunch Sun.*

$$ ✕ **Malee's on Main.** This fashionable eatery serves up sophisticated, Thai-inspired fare. Especially recommended is *Ahoi Phannee*, a medley of seafood in a bamboo-leaf bowl moistened with red curry sauce redolent of coconut, lime leaf, and Thai basil. The Thai barbecued chicken, grilled to a sizzle and coated with rum, is outstanding. Beware: take Malee's spices seriously—even the "mild" dishes have a bite. ✉ *7131 E. Main St.,* ☎ *602/947–6042. AE, DC, MC, V. No lunch Sun.*

Breakfast and Brunch

$$$$ ✕ **Terrace Dining Room.** The Phoenician's Terrace Dining
★ Room serves the most lavish (and expensive) Sunday brunch in town. Attention is paid to every detail, from the wheel of costly Parmigiano-Reggiano cheese to the fresh artichoke hearts in the salad. First, wander around the sushi section, the jumbo shrimp table, the homemade pastas, the pâtés, the crepes, and the blintzes and waffles. Then stroll to the main dishes: salmon and lamb chops are fired up on the grill, while filet mignon and pork tenderloin in port sauce are warmed in trays. Save room for desserts like homemade ice cream, elegant chocolate truffles, or pear-rhubarb tart. Mumm's Cuvee Napa keeps the meal bubbling, so don't plan anything more strenuous than a nap for the afternoon. ✉ *6000 E. Camelback Rd. (The Phoenician),* ☎ *602/423–2530. Reservations essential. AE, D, DC, MC, V.*

$$$ ✕ **Golden Swan.** This desert oasis is a great place for a leisurely Sunday champagne brunch. Sit outside under umbrellas or in a covered pavilion that juts into a koi-filled lagoon ringed by palms and hibiscus. The Golden Swan has a unique brunch schtick: everything except dessert is laid out in the kitchen under the watchful eyes of toque-clad chefs. Try the veal tortellini in lobster sauce, giant prawns, or filet mignon. ✉ *7500 E. Doubletree Ranch Rd. (Hyatt Regency at Gainey Ranch),* ☎ *602/991–3388. Reservations essential. AE, D, DC, MC, V.*

$ ✕ **Original Pancake House.** This breakfast landmark does one thing, and does it extremely well—pancakes. These flapjacks inspire worship from local admirers who wait patiently for a table on weekends. Chief among the griddled glories is the signature apple pancake: homemade batter is poured over sautéed apples and partially baked. Then the concoction is flipped over, glazed with cinnamon sugar and baked some more. It's creamy, sweet, bubbly . . . and huge. Other varieties, like the German pancake, are also exceptional. ⊠ *6840 E. Camelback Rd.,* ☎ *602/946–4902. Reservations not accepted. No credit cards.*

Continental

$$$$ ✕ **Mary Elaine's.** Swanky, formal, and austerely elegant, ★ Mary Elaine's is the Phoenician's showcase restaurant. Look out the big picture windows for a sweeping view of Phoenix, then edge into dinner with roasted langoustines and saffron risotto, veal sweetbreads, or seared foie gras with spiced pineapple and 100-year-old Balsamico. The main dishes such as maple-glazed squab, monkfish medallions, and veal tenderloin should please the most demanding patrons. ⊠ *6000 E. Camelback Rd. (The Phoenician),* ☎ *602/941–8200. Reservations essential. Jacket required. AE, D, DC, MC, V. Closed Sun. No lunch.*

French

$$$ ✕ **Cafe Patou.** The hearty French cuisine here is prepared with flair and skill. Appetizers range from the rustic charcuterie platter—duck pâté, prosciutto, sausage, cheese, olives, and cornichons—to the scallops and baked semolina in balsamic vinegar sauce. Vigorous appetites will appreciate entrées like the venison Stroganoff, filet mignon, and pork tenderloin stuffed with shrimp and covered with lobster sauce. If you prefer something simpler (and cheaper), try the superb crepes or the flat breads gilded with toppings like escargots, roasted vegetables, or olives and anchovies. ⊠ *7000 E. Shea Blvd.,* ☎ *602/951–6868. AE, D, DC, MC, V.*

International

$$$ ✕ **Marco Polo Supper Club.** Marco Polo proves that, contrary to popular belief, east and west do meet. Some of the unique dishes include filet mignon broccoli steak, a winning combination of prime beef, broccoli, and mushrooms stir-fried in a hoisin oyster sauce; Hong Kong chicken stuffed with cheese, shrimp, bean sprouts, and spinach over noodles; and lobster and shrimp pasta with thick Asian noodles in a spicy marinara sauce. The setting is as sophisticated as the fare with lots of polished brass and live music. ⊠ *8608 E. Shea Blvd.,* ☎ *602/483–1900. AE, DC, MC, V. No lunch.*

$$$ ✕ **Razz's Restaurant and Bar.** There's no telling what part of the globe chef-proprietor Erasmo "Razz" Kamnitzer will use for culinary inspiration. However, you can count on his creations to give dormant taste buds a wake-up call: black bean paella is a twist on a Spanish theme; South American bouillabaisse is a fragrant fish stew, stocked with veggies; and *bah mie goreng* teams noodles with fish, meat, and vegetables, perked up with dried cranberries and almonds. Count on it—Razz'll dazzle. ⊠ *10321 N. Scottsdale Rd.,* ☎ *602/905–1308. AE, DC, MC, V. Closed Sun. and Mon. No lunch.*

$$ ✕ **L'Ecole.** You'll have no regrets putting yourself in the talented hands of the student-chefs at the Valley's premier cooking academy. You get a three-course dinner for about $20, a real bargain. Look for inventive appetizers like ginger soy gravlax, and main dishes like fillet Rossini. Because the students also pull server duty, you can count on being pampered, too. ⊠ *8100 E. Camelback Rd. (Scottsdale Culinary Institute),* ☎ *602/990–7639. Reservations essential. D, MC, V. Closed weekends.*

Italian

$$$ ✕ **Franco's Trattoria.** The Florence-born Franco puts together ★ meals that sing with the flavors of Tuscany. Start with focaccia and hunks of imported Italian cheeses sliced off huge wheels. Next, sample the antipasto or the tasty risotto. Main dishes are hearty and vibrant; naturally, veal is a specialty: the *orecchie d'elefante* (so named because it seems as massive as an elephant's ear) is pounded to millimeter thinness, breaded, fried, and splayed across the plate, coated with tomatoes and shallots, basil, and lemon. ⊠ *8120 N. Hayden Rd.,* ☎ *602/948–6655. AE, MC, V. Closed Sun. and July. No lunch.*

$$–$$$ ✕ **Maria's When in Naples.** In a town teeming with Italian restaurants, this is a standout. The antipasto spread laid out just inside the entrance is sure to grab your attention, and it tastes as good as it looks. The homemade pasta is another winner. Check out the *salsiccia Pugliese* (fettuccine topped with homemade sausage, leeks, porcini mushrooms, and white wine sauce), or the *orecchiette Barese* (ear-shape pasta tossed with cauliflower, pancetta, sun-dried tomatoes, olive oil, and cheese). ⊠ *7000 E. Shea Blvd.,* ☎ *602/991–6887. AE, D, DC, MC, V. No lunch weekends.*

$$–$$$ ✕ **Veneto Trattoria.** This restaurant is a delightful neighborhood spot, aimed at locals in a tony area of Scottsdale that caters mostly to tourists. The kitchen specializes in rustic Venetian fare: duck breast, spruced up with duck liver and smoked pork; *luganega,* juicy, garlicky pork sausages teamed with polenta and braised Savoy cabbage; and *bollito di manzo,* boiled beef paired with two horseradish sauces. The semifreddo dessert—semifrozen meringue studded with dried fruit and pine nuts, drizzled with chocolate sauce and a raspberry coulis, sends you home with a big grin. ⊠ *6137 N. Scottsdale Rd. (Hilton Village),* ☎ *602/ 948–9928. AE, D, DC, MC, V. Closed Sun.*

$ ✕ **Oregano's.** This happening, jam-packed pizza-pasta-sandwich parlor lures customers with two irresistible come-ons: good food and low prices. Oregano's offers two types of Chicago pizza: stuffed deep-dish and thin-crust, and both are great. So are the untraditional lasagna, particularly the artichoke one, made with whole-wheat pasta (it's worth the 30-minute wait). Sandwich fans will appreciate the baked Italian hoagie, stuffed with pepperoni, capicolla, salami, and provolone, then loaded with tomatoes, onions, peppers, and olives. ⊠ *3622 N. Scottsdale Rd.,* ☎ *602/970–1860. Reservations not accepted. AE, D, MC, V.*

Mexican

$$$ ✕ **La Hacienda.** The food here is nothing like the run-
★ from-the-border fare you find at neighborhood taco stands—it's more like the food of Mexico's colonial grandee. The appetizers, such as a mushroom crepe enlivened with *huitlacoche* (a fungus of almost trufflelike intensity), are stunning. The entrées are heavy with seafood: huge, grilled Gulf shrimp; red snapper in a Veracruzana sauce; lightly seared ahi tuna, encrusted with potatoes. *Cochinillo asado* is La Hacienda's signature dish—roast suckling pig, wheeled up to the table and carved to order. Finish with *cajeta* ice-cream crepes or the mesmerizing pumpkin-chocolate cheese-

cake. ⊠ 7575 E. Princess Dr. (Scottsdale Princess Resort), ☎ 602/585–4848. AE, D, DC, MC, V. No lunch.

$–$$ ✕ **Carlsbad Tavern.** This is Mexican food served New Mexican style, which means dishes with a hot-chili bite. Get yourself a potent frozen margarita (there's a nice selection of premium tequilas) to wash down starters like red chili potato pancakes and ravioli stuffed with smoked duck and tequila-marinated grilled shrimp. Entrées continue the flavor assault: *carne adovada* is pork simmered in red chili sauce; the *machaca* tamale duo features two shredded beef tamales, one in green chili sauce, the other coated with spicy red chili; and lamb pierna, a wood-grilled, braised leg of lamb topped with red wine sauce. ⊠ 3315 N. Hayden Rd., ☎ 602/970–8156. Reservations not accepted. AE, D, DC, MC, V.

Middle Eastern

$–$$ ✕ **Al Amir.** Along with traditional appetizer favorites like *baba ghanoush* (mashed eggplant), hummus, falafel, and tabbouleh, this spot serves *ma'anek,* juicy Lebanese sausages zinged with cloves, and *safiha,* canape-size pockets of dough stuffed with ground lamb. Main dishes feature kabobs, but it pays to explore the less familiar options. The *kebbe bil sanyeh* is sensational with layers of heavily seasoned ground beef baked with bulgur wheat and pine nuts. Don't leave without ordering *knafeh,* a warm cheese pastry smothered in syrup. ⊠ 8989 E. Via Linda, ☎ 602/661–1137. AE, D, MC, V. Closed Sun.

Seafood

$$$$ ✕ **Restaurant Oceana.** When you're 400 mi from the nearest ocean, you can expect to pay for your seafood thrills. You'll pay at Restaurant Oceana, but you'll also get plenty of thrills. Everything here was swimming in the sea 24 hours ago. The daily-changing menu may include scallops the size of hockey pucks, Casco Bay cod, Belon oysters from Washington, and mahimahi. Gingerbread cake with an apple cider sabayon, macadamia nut-honey square with chocolate truffle ice cream, and chocolate cake with a molten chocolate center are just three can't-miss desserts. ⊠ 8900 E. Pinnacle Peak Rd., ☎ 602/515–2277. AE, D, DC, MC, V. No lunch.

Southwestern

$$$–
$$$$
✕ **Pinon Grill.** Delicious southwestern fare is served up in a rustic, woodsy atmosphere. Try not to fill up on the green chili corn bread as you'll need to save room for flavorful regional dishes. Every restaurant in town serves grilled ahi tuna, but no one else fires it up with a dreamy red jalapeño basil sauce and cools it down with melon salsa. Either the rich chocolate taco or intense chocolate pâté ends the meal on a high note. ⊠ *7401 N. Scottsdale Rd. (Inn at Regal McCormick Ranch),* ☎ *602/948–5050. AE, D, DC, MC, V.*

$$$
★
✕ **Cafe Terra Cotta.** This Scottsdale branch of the acclaimed Tucson original shows you how the Southwest was won using inventive regional creations and sophisticated flavors. Start off with buffalo carpaccio drizzled with chili-infused oil or a quesadilla filled with duck and smoked Gouda cheese. Next, move to lamb chops in an ancho-chili mole or salmon crusted with sunflower seeds and yellow chili sauce. Desserts are just as formidable, especially the orange-curd tart. ⊠ *6166 N. Scottsdale Rd. (Borgata Shopping Center),* ☎ *602/948–8100. AE, D, DC, MC, V.*

Spanish

$$$–
$$$$
★
✕ **Marquesa.** This gem of a restaurant pays homage to Catalonia, the region around Barcelona. Everything here is right on target, from the setting to the service. Appetizers are extraordinary: *Anec D'Napoleon,* phyllo dough pouches stuffed with a heady blend of duck, foie gras, and mushrooms; and *pebrots del piquillo,* crab and fontina cheese baked into sweet red peppers. Main dishes include monkfish-veal loin duo; pan-roasted rack of lamb; and a first-class paella crammed with lobster, shrimp, mussels, clams, chicken, and *chistora* (a sharp Spanish sausage). For dessert, the Gran Torres cheesecake and flan are equally wonderful. ⊠ *7575 E. Princess Dr. (Scottsdale Princess Resort),* ☎ *602/585–4848. Reservations essential. AE, D, DC, MC, V. No lunch.*

North Central Phoenix

American

$$$–
$$$$
✕ **Morton's.** This national steak-house chain doesn't stint on quality and doesn't believe in menus: you have to sit through a 10-minute recital by your server to find out

what's served. The New York sirloin is what beef is all about, a ravishing 20-ounce strip that perfectly packages looks, taste and texture, and the juicy 24-ounce porterhouse is heart-stopping. The à la carte side dishes are big enough to split two or three ways, but if you have room for dessert try the chocolate Godiva cake, a moist sponge cake with a molten chocolate interior. ✉ *2425 E. Camelback Rd. (Shops at the Esplanade),* ☎ *602/955–9577. AE, DC, MC, V. No lunch.*

$$$ ✕ **El Chorro Lodge.** Near the Phoenix Mountains Preserve, El Chorro has been doing business in this picturesque location for 60 years. Sit outside, gaze at the mountains and stars, and try not to make a meal of the famous sticky buns that immediately come to your table. El Chorro's forte is prime-graded meat. Beef Stroganoff, top sirloin, and the chateaubriand for two are tops, and fresh ocean fare like orange roughy and swordfish are also skillfully prepared. The dense chocolate-chip pecan pie makes dessert a must. ✉ *5550 E. Lincoln Dr.,* ☎ *602/948–5170. AE, D, DC, MC, V.*

$$ ✕ **Texaz Grill.** The down-home fare here is served in a cowboy setting that oozes with neighborhood charm. The T-bone steak and butter-soft fillet are very satisfying, but it's the he-man-size chicken-fried steak that lures most folks here. The fork-tender beef is encased in crisp batter and ladled with thick, peppery country gravy; the mashed potato side—with the skin mashed in—is a worthy accompaniment. Order yourself a Lone Star brew, put some coins in the jukebox, and loosen your belt. ✉ *6003 N. 16th St.,* ☎ *602/248–7827. Reservations not accepted. AE, MC, V. No lunch Sun.*

Asian

$$$ ✕ **ObaChine.** Celebrity-chef Wolfgang Puck's lavishly decorated place—there's enough Asian art here to stock a small museum—is as interesting to contemplate as his take on pan-Asian cuisine. Try the fabulous warm sesame-crusted oysters to start things off. Entrées, served family-style, include an intriguing noodle dish tossed with quail; tea-smoked duck with scallion crepes; and a beautiful platter of seared tuna slices with Chinese eggplant and black-eyed peas. Desserts aren't really Asian, but they're good: banana spring rolls—battered bananas, deep-fried and teamed with candied walnuts and caramel rum sauce—make the point. ⊠ *2500 E. Camelback Rd. (Biltmore Fashion Park),* ☎ *602/955–9653. AE, DC, MC, V.*

$–$$ ✕ **China Village.** This place doesn't pretend to be anything more than it is: a neighborhood spot dishing out traditional Chinese fare. However, the old favorites are prepared better here than just about anyplace else. Favorites include the tangerine beef, lemon chicken, twice-cooked pork, and the yui-shan eggplant, a dish with skin-on, cooked-to-a-pulp eggplant laced with minced pork and seasoned with ginger, garlic, and hot chilies. ⊠ *12005 N. 32nd St.,* ☎ *602/ 953–1961. AE, D, DC, MC, V.*

Breakfast and Brunch

$–$$ ✕ **Chompie's Deli.** Run by Brooklyn refugees, this bustling deli brings a bite of the Big Apple to Phoenix with its smoked fish, blintzes, homemade cream cheeses, and herring in cream sauce. The outstanding bagels will remind New York expats of home—about 20 varieties are baked fresh daily. There's also a top-notch bakery on the premises, with rugalach, pies, and coffee cake. Bring a newspaper, or schmooze with your pals. Sometimes you have to stop and smell the bagels. ⊠ *3202 E. Greenway Rd.,* ☎ *602/971– 8010. Reservations not accepted. AE, MC, V.*

French/Continental

$$$$ ✕ **Chaparral Restaurant.** Discerning diners who appreci-
  ★   ate classic fare will be delighted by the tuxedoed staff, the elegant decor, and the timeless menu. Starters include rich lobster bisque with a puff-pastry cap topped with caviar and crème fraîche. For your main course, all the standards are offered: Beef Wellington, Veal Oscar, Steak Diane, and Sole Meuniere. There aren't too many places left that know their way around these dishes. Dress up, and make believe it's 1958. ⊠ *5402 E. Lincoln Dr. (Marriott's Camelback Inn),* ☎ *602/948–6644. Reservations essential. AE, D, DC, MC, V. No lunch.*

$$$ ✕ **Bistro 24.** Smart, stylish, and sophisticated, Bistro 24 has a Gallic accent in the kitchen to go with its parquet floor, colorful murals, and snazzy bar. Mussels steamed in champagne make a lively first course, and the main dishes tilt toward seafood. Grilled salmon, bouillabaisse, and crispy-skin whitefish are deftly done, as is the steak au poivre, served with French-style *frites*. Finish up with a soufflé of tarte Tatin, and rich French-press coffee. Sunday brunch is outstanding. ⊠ *2401 E. Camelback Rd. (Ritz-Carlton Hotel). AE, D, DC, MC, V.*

Greek

$$–$$$ ✗ **Greekfest.** This pretty place with whitewashed walls feels like an island taverna and brings the flavors of the Aegean to life. Among the appetizers, look for *taramosalata* (mullet roe blended with lemon and olive oil) and *saganaki* (*kefalograviera* cheese flamed with brandy and extinguished with a squirt of lemon). Entrées, many featuring lamb and shrimp, are equally hard-hitting. Try *exohiko* (chunks of lamb mixed with eggplant, peppers, zucchini, and mushrooms). For dessert, the *galaktoboureko* (warm custard pie baked in phyllo dough and scented with cloves and honey) is a triumph of western civilization. ⊠ *1940 E. Camelback Rd.,* ☎ *602/265–2990. AE, D, DC, MC, V. No lunch Sun.*

Indian

$$ ✗ **Taste of India.** Bread is one of the tests of an Indian kitchen, and the models here—bhatura, naan, paratha, poori—are superb. Just about every spice in the rack is used for dishes like lamb kashmiry and tandoori chicken. Vegetarians will enjoy this spot's wonderful meatless specialties, including *benghan bhartha*, fashioned from eggplant, or *bhindi masala*, a tempting okra dish. Indian desserts include fragrant *ras malai*, a Bengali treat of sweet milk and cheese, with bits of pistachio. ⊠ *1609 E. Bell Rd.,* ☎ *602/ 788–3190. AE, D, MC, V.*

International

$$$–
$$$$ ✗ **Tarbell's.** Sure it's sleek, smart, and glitzy, but Tarbell's distinguishes itself from the trendoid pack with deftly prepared dishes. The menu changes daily, but you can usually find the vibrant smoked rock shrimp starter. If they're available, order the aromatic mussels, steamed in a heady broth of white wine and shallots. Pricier entrées include a first-rate New York steak with *pommes frites*; on the low end, there's surprisingly good pizza. Your sweet tooth won't be neglected if you opt for the rich Hawaiian chocolate mousse. ⊠ *3213 E. Camelback Rd.,* ☎ *602/955– 8100. AE, D, DC, MC, V. No lunch.*

$$$ ✕ **Lon's at the Hermosa.** A beautifully restored 1930s
★   adobe inn with wood-beamed ceilings and beehive fireplaces,
Lon's has a rustic Old Arizona feel, but the menu spans the
globe. Appetizers may include grilled polenta pie with wild
mushroom ragout, ravioli filled with vegetables and goat
cheese, or garlic prawns with pineapple relish. Many of the
main dishes are grilled over wood: loin of pork, filet mignon,
rack of lamb, ahi tuna, and salmon. Pasta, chicken, duck,
and veal are other standouts. For dessert, look for the gin-
gered crème brûlée tart or chocolate truffle pâté. ✉ *5532
N. Palo Cristi Dr. (Hermosa Inn),* ☎ *602/955–7878. AE,
D, DC, MC, V. No lunch weekends.*

$$$ ✕ **RoxSand.** With a quirky, risky, and imaginative culinary
★   flair, Chef RoxSand Scocos doesn't follow trends; she sets
them at one of the most interesting restaurants in the state.
Who else would think to stuff tamales with curried lamb
moistened in a Thai-style peanut sauce? The heavenly
b'stilla is a Moroccan-inspired appetizer of braised chicken
in phyllo dough, covered with almonds and powdered
sugar, and specials like mango and wild rice soup tap taste
buds you didn't know you had. Air-dried duck is an exotic
house specialty, served with buckwheat crepes and a pis-
tachio-onion marmalade. Feta-stuffed chicken breast with
polenta-fried shrimp is another offbeat success. Desserts are
wicked, especially the B-52 torte, an intoxicating disk of
chocolate laced with Kahlua and Bailey's. ✉ *2594 E.
Camelback Rd. (Biltmore Fashion Park),* ☎ *602/381–
0444. AE, DC, MC, V.*

Italian

$$$– ✕ **Il Forno.** This is one of the nicest-looking places in town
$$$$ with cherry wood, sleek, shiny mirrors, and eye-catching
prints, and the contemporary Italian fare is just as attrac-
tive. Chicken breast stuffed with wild mushrooms, figs and
plums, moistened by a sweet white wine sauce, is one of
the town's best entrées. Rack of lamb and the seafood stew
in a lobster and white wine broth both shine. So does the
pappardelle alla Bolognese, wide pasta ribbons bathed in
a dreamy veal sauce. In a town bursting with Italian restau-
rants, Il Forno is one of only a handful of standouts. ✉ *4225
E. Camelback,* ☎ *602/952–1522. AE, MC, V. No lunch.*

Mexican/Latin American

$$–$$$ ✗ **Havana Patio Cafe.** This Cuban and Latin-American restaurant says "Yanqui, come back" with its flavorful but not too spicy fare. Appetizers are marvelous, particularly the shrimp pancakes, potato croquettes, and Cuban tamale. The best main dishes are the *ropa vieja,* shredded braised beef served with *moros,* a blend of black beans and rice; *pollo Cubano,* chicken breast marinated in lime, orange, and garlic; and *mariscos con salsa verde,* shellfish simmered in a traditional green sauce. Vegetarians will adore the *causa azulada,* a Peruvian platter featuring a blue mashed-potato cake layered with carrot and served on Swiss chard. ⊠ *6245 E. Bell Rd.,* ☎ *602/991–1496. AE, D, DC, MC, V. Closed Mon.*

$$ ✗ **Richardson's.** This neighborhood haunt can be noisy and the waitstaff surly, but the fiery fugue of flavors known as New Mexican–style still packs 'em in until midnight. Loose-cushioned adobe booths surround three sides of a lively bar, and an open kitchen turns out chilies rellenos, enchiladas, and other first-rate standbys. Shrimp, chicken, and chops come off the pecan wood burning grill with distinctive, savory undertones; Chimayo chicken is flavorfully stuffed with spinach, dried tomatoes, poblano chilies, and asiago cheese, and served with a twice-baked green chili potato. There's a wait on weekends, so don't expect to linger at the table after dinner. ⊠ *1582 E. Bethany Home Rd.,* ☎ *602/265–5886. AE, MC, V.*

$ ✗ **Blue Burrito Grille.** "Healthy Mexican food" used to be an oxymoron, but not anymore. Here you can find good-for-you, south-of-the-border fare without the lard but with all the taste. Among the heart-healthy menu items are chicken burritos, fish tacos, tamales Mexicanos, enchiladas rancheras, vegetarian burritos, and outstanding blue corn vegetarian tacos. ⊠ *3118 E. Camelback Rd.,* ☎ *602/ 955–9596. Reservations not accepted. AE, MC, V.*

$ ✗ **El Bravo.** The principal decor motif at this spot is the col-
★ lage of bad checks posted by the "Order Here" window. But cognoscenti of Mexican food won't care about the decorating lapses; they come for the town's best Sonoran fare. (Sonora is the Mexican state that borders Arizona.) Burros here are edible works of art, like the *machaca* (shredded beef) *burro.* Enchiladas, chimichangas, and tacos are

just as thrilling. If you've got a taste for chili zest, try the red beef popover—it will leave your tongue tingling. Even the sweets are outstanding. Go for the chocolate chimichanga—it's like a creamy Mexican s'more. ⊠ *8338 N. 7th St.,* ☎ *602/943–9753. Reservations not accepted. No credit cards.*

Southwestern

$$$–
$$$$
★

✕ **Vincent Guerithault on Camelback.** It's hard to tell whether chef Guerithault prepares French food with a southwestern flair, or southwestern fare with a French touch. But whatever this talented chef prepares will be incredibly tempting. Make a meal of the famous appetizers: the duck tamale, smoked salmon quesadilla, and chipotle lobster ravioli are all ravishing. Main dishes are just as strong. The duck confit, rack of lamb, and grilled wild boar loin make choosing difficult, and the sautéed veal sweetbreads with blue cornmeal are out-of-this-world. The signature crème brûlée arrives in three, thin pastry cups filled with vanilla, coffee, and coconut custard. ⊠ *3930 E. Camelback Rd.,* ☎ *602/224–0225. Reservations essential. AE, D, DC, MC, V. No lunch weekends.*

$$

✕ **Sam's Cafe.** This is the southwestern restaurant that locals bring their skittish Midwestern relatives to with perfect confidence. Nothing's too far out, but most everything is interesting and tasty. The fragrant poblano chicken chowder is fine, as are the Sedona spring rolls, flour tortillas wrapped around chicken and veggies, with a chipotle barbecue sauce. The hands-down main dish winner is the inventive chicken-fried tuna, a lightly battered slab adorned with a jalapeño cream gravy, served with chili-mashed potatoes. Steaks, chops, tacos, and pastas (try the chicken pasta, flamed with tequila) are outstanding, and the chilled flan, fashioned from yams, drizzled with caramel sauce and garnished with pecans, is worth a dessert splurge. ⊠ *2566 E. Camelback Rd. (Biltmore Fashion Park),* ☎ *602/ 954–7100. AE, D, DC, MC, V.*

Spanish

$$–$$$

✕ **Altos.** This hot spot attracts sophisticated locals who bask in the scents of Iberia—garlic, sherry, olive oil, saffron. Calamari de Pedro (tender squid dipped in a saffron batter and sizzled in olive oil) is a good appetizer for sharing. *Som-*

brilla Andaluza is mesmerizing, a portobello mushroom marinated in olive oil, garlic and sherry, then grilled and festooned with red cabbage, parsley, and Serrano ham. Main dishes are also invigorating. The *filete pelon* is a buttery filet mignon topped with cabrales, a creamy Spanish blue cheese. *Lomo en adobo* is pork loin, smothered in a lusty sauce with hints of chili, sesame seeds, sugar, and peanuts. The sugar-glazed chocolate espresso crème brûlée may be the single best dessert in Arizona. ⊠ *5029 N. 44th St.,* ☎ *602/808–0890. AE, D, DC, MC, V. No lunch weekends.*

Central Phoenix

American

$$$ ✕ **Eddie's Grill.** Chef Eddie Matney's "New American"
★ menu livens up traditional dishes in unexpected ways. The restaurant's signature platter, seared New York steak with potatoes, is not the same old beef and spuds: it's a beautiful sirloin strip encased in a mashed-potato crust, dusted with Parmesan and Romano cheeses, then lightly fried and topped with a cabernet demi-glace. Likewise, the mango and five-peppercorn-coated chicken breast, served over roasted plantain and chili mashed potatoes, is hardly your typical poultry snoozer. The seafood cioppino potpie—shellfish in a fennel-flavored broth with a puff pastry crust—is irresistible. The lively, sophisticated setting is another plus. ⊠ *4747 N. 7th St.,* ☎ *602/241–1188. AE, D, DC, MC, V. No lunch weekends.*

$$–$$$ ✕ **Oyster Grill.** At the Oyster Grill, you may think you hear the sounds of seagulls overhead. The daily menu lets you know that fish is fresh that day, and there's only one method of preparation: grilled over alder wood. If you have adventurous tastes, you'll enjoy the Sonoran oyster curry stew (plump bluepoints in a spicy, curry-tinged cream broth with eggplant, onions, and crispy fried leeks). Along with an oyster bar, there's a full-scale dining room. ⊠ *455 N. 3rd St. (Arizona Center),* ☎ *602/252–6767. AE, D, DC, MC, V.*

$$ ✕ **Steamed Blues.** Crabs in the desert? No, it's not a mirage. This restaurant specializes in blue crabs that are still swimming when you order them. Prepare for the din of pounding mallets as diners attack their dinner—you might think you're in the middle of the "Anvil Chorus" scene in

"Il Trovatore." If you prefer not to hammer your meal, there are soft-shell crabs, as well as crab cakes and steamed shrimp. The "Boardwalk" fries—fresh-cut, seasoned, sizzling potatoes—will make you think you're on a Chesapeake Bay pier. ⊠ *4843 N. 8th Pl.,* ☎ *602/966–2722. Reservations not accepted. AE, D, DC, MC, V. No lunch weekends.*

$$ ✕ **T-Bone Steak House.** You won't see staged gunfights or Indian dances at T-Bone Steak House. You'll just see seriously good steaks in a ranch-house setting. The small menu sticks to the basics: a monstrous 2-pound porterhouse, a 1-pound T-bone, and 12-ounce sirloin, all of them juicy and flavorful. Another bonus: the view. The restaurant sits about halfway up South Mountain. Come at dusk for a great look at the twinkling city lights below. ⊠ *10037 S. 19th Ave.,* ☎ *602/276–0945. AE, DC, MC, V. No lunch.*

$ ✕ **Honey Bear's BBQ.** Honey Bear's motto—"You don't need no teeth to eat our meat"—may fall short on grammar, but this place isn't packed with folks looking to improve their language skills. If you've got barbecue fever, the meaty pork ribs are the cure. This is Tennessee-style barbecue, which means smoky baby backs basted in thick, zippy, slightly sweet sauce with a wonderful orange tang. The sausage-enhanced "cowbro" beans and scallion-studded potato salad are great sides. If a slab of ribs still leaves you hungry, finish up with the homemade sweet potato pie. ⊠ *5012 E. Van Buren St.,* ☎ *602/273–9148. Reservations not accepted. AE, D, MC, V.*

$ ✕ **Mrs. White's Golden Rule Cafe.** You can get second-hand arteriosclerosis just walking past this landmark soul food parlor. Look for chicken-fried steak so tender you can dispense with your knife; oversize pork chops in a fried crust; heavenly Southern-fried chicken that will make you proud to be nutritionally incorrect; and lovely smothered chicken, battered poultry heaped with a thick, country gravy. Why "Golden Rule" Cafe? At the end of the meal, just tell the cashier what you had—your conscience and your belly will both be happy. ⊠ *808 E. Jefferson,* ☎ *602/262–9256. Reservations not accepted. No credit cards. Closed weekends. No dinner.*

Asian

$–$$ ✕ **Gourmet House of Hong Kong.** This popular Chinese restaurant draws customers who are interested in genuine

Chinatown specialties like *chow fun* (thick rice noodles). Try the assorted meat version, topped with chicken, shrimp, pork, and squid. Lobster with black bean sauce may be the world's messiest platter, but it's also one of the tastiest. Don't wear anything that needs to be dry-cleaned. Along with an extensive seafood list, adventurous delights like five-flavor frogs' legs, duck feet with greens, and beef tripe casserole are offered. ✉ *1438 E. McDowell Rd.,* ☎ *602/253–4859. AE, D, DC, MC, V.*

Italian

$$$–
$$$$
✕ **Avanti.** More than two decades old, this swanky place with its mirrored black-and-chrome interior still has old-fashioned elegance. So does the food. The proprietors have spent the last 20 years fine-tuning the standard Italian-Continental repertoire. Homemade pasta makes a wonderful first course, particularly the gnocchi and spinach ravioli. Standard entrées like veal chops, cioppino, and shrimp in a brandy-garlic sauce still deliver a powerful sensory experience. Give Avanti credit for refusing to keep up with the times and not confusing change for progress. ✉ *2728 E. Thomas, Rd.,* ☎ *602/956–0900, AE, D, DC, MC, V. No lunch weekends.*

$$–$$$
★
✕ **La Fontanella.** This outstanding neighborhood Italian restaurant is a winning combination of quality and value. The mom-and-pop proprietors deliver all the hard-hitting flavors of their native land: *suppli,* a Roman specialty, rice croquettes filled with cheese; and escargots, bubbling in garlic and butter get the meal off to a fast start. All the entrées are first-rate; some are out-of-this-world. Among the latter are lamb *agrassato,* lamb shank braised in wine with raisins, pine nuts, and potatoes; osso buco, gilded with pancetta; seafood *reale,* shrimp and scallops in a sherry cream sauce; and the herb-crusted rack of lamb. For dessert, La Fontanella's homemade gelato puts an exclamation mark on dinner. ✉ *4231 E. Indian School Rd.,* ☎ *602/955–1213. AE, D, DC, MC, V. No lunch weekends.*

$–$$
★
✕ **Pizzeria Bianco.** Bronx-native Chris Bianco makes pizza good enough to inspire memories of Naples, even if you've never been there. The secret? A wood-fired brick oven and a passion for quality. Bianco's pizza crust is a work of art, not too bready, not too light, and just chewy enough to keep your jaws happy. Toppings include imported cheeses, home-

made fennel sausage, wood-roasted cremini mushrooms, and the freshest herbs and spices. There's also antipasto and sandwiches on fresh-baked bread. ⊠ *623 E. Adams St.,* ☎ *602/258–8300. MC, V. Closed Mon. No lunch weekends.*

Mexican/Latin American

$$–$$$ ✕ **Such Is Life.** No gringo touches here: authentic, Yucatan-
★ inspired Mexican fare keeps the place packed. For starters, try the *nopal polanco,* a prickly pear cactus pad topped with Chihuahua cheese and chorizo. The lusty, lemon-tinged chicken soup is also thick with poultry, avocado, and hard-boiled egg. Entrées include chicken mole and adobo pork, simmered in a fragrant ancho chili, sesame-orange sauce. If the kitchen has Gulf shrimp, get them grilled in garlic. ⊠ *3602 N. 24th St.,* ☎ *602/955–7822. Reservations essential. AE, D, DC, MC, V. Closed Sun. No lunch Sat.*

$$ ✕ **San Carlos Bay Seafood Restaurant.** From the street, San
★ Carlos Bay doesn't look like much, but the best Mexican seafood in town is served inside. Start off with a seafood cocktail teeming with octopus or shrimp, in a riveting tomato-based liquid spiked with onions, cilantro, lime, and pepper. Among the main dishes, the Veracruz-style filleted snapper is coated with olives, onions, tomatoes, and peppers. The delicious, meaty crustaceans come soaked in a devilishly hot sauce. For seafood that doesn't make your nostrils flare, try the well-stocked Seven Seas stew. ⊠ *1901 E. McDowell Rd.,* ☎ *602/340–0892. Reservations not accepted. No credit cards.*

$–$$ ✕ **Los Dos Molinos.** Is this the place that launched a thou-
★ sand chips? You bet it is. This restaurant features New-Mexican–style Mexican food. For the uninitiated, that means HOT!—you'll know after one bite. Legions of heat seekers practically worship the Hatch, New Mexico, chilies that form the backbone of the dishes here. Adobada ribs, a specialty, feature fall-off-the-bone meat marinated in red chilies, and the green chili enchilada and beef taco are potentially lethal. But there's flavor in this fire. The *sopaipilla,* a pillow of fried dough doused with cinnamon, honey, or powdered sugar, is the New Mexican antidote to chili flames, but if you can't stand the heat, stay out of this kitchen. ⊠ *8646 S. Central Ave.,* ☎ *602/243–9113. Reservations not accepted. AE, D, MC, V. Closed Mon.*

$ ✕ **Eliana's Restaurant.** This simple, family-run ethnic gem features budget-priced El Salvadoran specialties skillfully prepared. You can make a meal of the appetizers: *pupusas* (corn patties stuffed with pork, peppers, and cheese); *pasteles* (meat turnovers); and tamales, filled with chicken and vegetables. Main dishes will wipe out hunger pangs for about the price of a movie ticket. There's *pollo encebollado* (fried chicken with rice and beans), and *mojarra frita*, a whole fried tilapia, an Arizona farm-raised fish popular in Latin America. You can wash your meal down with refreshing homemade fruit drinks. ⊠ *1627 N. 24th St.,* ☎ *602/225–2925. Reservations not accepted. AE, D, MC, V. Closed Mon.*

East Valley: Tempe, Mesa, Chandler

American

$$$–   ✕ **Top of the Rock.** The iron law of restaurant physics proclaims that food quality declines the higher off the ground you get. (Airline food is the ultimate proof.) But Top of the Rock seems to be the exception to the rule. This beautiful room, set atop a Tempe butte, has panoramic views of the Valley and food that is simply tops. The lobster Napoleon appetizer—lobster layered between crispy wontons lined with Boursin cheese—is good enough to order for entrée and dessert. Main dishes include sugar-spiced barbecue salmon, roasted veal chop, free-range chicken, and mesquite-grilled Black Angus sirloin steak. The house specialty dessert is black bottom pie, with a chocolate praline center and chocolate mousse topping. This is a great spot for a romantic dinner. ⊠ *2000 Westcourt Way (Buttes Resort), Tempe,* ☎ *602/225–9000. Reservations essential. AE, D, DC, MC, V. No lunch.*
$$$$ ★

Asian

$$–$$$ ✕ **Yamakasa.** Yamakasa, one of the Valley's top Japanese restaurants, and its next-door neighbor, C-Fu Gourmet, order their ocean fare in tandem, so you can be sure the high-quality sushi here is fresh. The skilled sushi masters display particular artistry in the hand rolls. Two nabemono (hot pot) dishes are also worth investigating. Another specialty is *shabu-shabu,* thin-sliced beef, swished in a boiling, sake-seasoned, vegetable-filled broth. ("Shabu-shabu" is the hissing sound the meat makes when it hits the liquid.) ⊠

2051 W. Warner, Chandler, ☎ *602/899–8868. AE, D, DC, MC, V. Closed Mon. No lunch Sun.*

$$ ✕ **C-Fu Gourmet.** This is serious Chinese food, the kind you'd
★ expect to find on Mott Street in New York City's China-
town or Grant Street in San Francisco. C-Fu's specialty is
fish, and you can see several species in big holding tanks.
If you've ever wondered why shrimp is a delicacy, it will
be clear once you bite into these crustaceans. After they're
fished out of the tank, they're steamed and bathed in a po-
tent garlic sauce. Clams in black bean sauce and tilapia in
a ginger-scallion sauce also hit all the right buttons. There's
a daily dim sum brunch, too. ⊠ *2051 W. Warner, Chan-
dler,* ☎ *602/899–3888. AE, D, DC, MC, V.*

French

$$–$$$ ✕ **Citrus Cafe.** The French proprietors of this café may not
boast a fancy Scottsdale address, but they serve some of the
best French fare in the Valley. The daily menu is printed on
a marker board according to what's fresh in the market.
Try the *feuilleté aux champignons* (mushrooms in puff
pastry) or duck pâté studded with pistachios. The main dishes
are pure French comfort food: veal kidneys, sweetbreads,
leg of lamb, roast pork, and occasionally even rabbit. For
dessert, there's *vacherin,* a marvelous mound of baked
meringue that you won't see anyplace else in town. ⊠
2330 N. Alma School Rd., Chandler, ☎ *602/899–0502.
AE, D, DC, MC, V. Closed Sun. and Mon. and Aug. No
lunch.*

German

$–$$ ✕ **Zur Kate.** An unpretentious delight with genuine "gemut-
lichkeit," this restaurant has a homey congeniality that no
interior designer can manufacture. The place is crammed
with beer steins, flags, travel posters and, on weekends, live
oom-pah-pah music. The menu covers traditional German
territory, which means lots of pork. Some of the favorites
are smoked pork chop, ground ham and pork loaf, breaded
pork cutlet, and homemade bratwurst. Side dishes are as
filling as they are tempting: potato dumplings, home fries,
tart potato salad, and pungent sauerkraut. ⊠ *4815 E.
Main St., Mesa,* ☎ *602/830–4244. Reservations not accepted. MC, V. Closed Sun. (Sun.–Mon. in summer).*

International

$$ ✕ **House of Tricks.** There's nothing up the sleeves of Robert and Robin Trick, the inventive chef-proprietors of this rustic-looking restaurant. The imaginative appetizer list is known for its offbeat creations, like cheese and avocado blintzes and stuffed grape leaves in chipotle plum sauce. The main dishes are equally clever. The roast eggplant and goat cheese lasagna is outstanding. Grilled rack of pork with a jalapeño-orange marmalade and scallops in a saffron Pernod sauce also get high marks. The patio bar is a pleasant place to pass a mild Valley evening. ⊠ *114 E. 7th St., Tempe,* ☎ *602/968–1114. AE, D, DC, MC, V. Closed Sun.*

$–$$ ✕ **Euro Cafe.** If this place had a motto, it would be "Nothing succeeds like excess" when it comes to portion size and flavor. The southern Mediterranean-theme fare is staggering, in every sense. The Chicken Palm dish, adorned with palm hearts and artichokes heaped over pasta, could feed a small army. The gyros platter, heaped with capers, sun-dried tomatoes, red peppers, and two kinds of Greek cheeses, is equally generous. And beware the penne carbonara, an unconscionable quantity of pasta tubes fattened with ham and bacon, drenched in a creamy cheese sauce. ⊠ *1111 S. Longmore, Mesa,* ☎ *602/962–4224. AE, D, DC, MC, V.*

Italian

$ ✕ **Organ Stop Pizza.** If you're towing around kids, this is the place for dinner. The centerpiece of the operation is the Mighty Wurlitzer Organ, with its 276 keys, 675 stops and 5,000 pipes. Organists provide continuous entertainment, while the family munches on Italian-American standards—pizza, pasta, sandwiches, and salads. It's all as corny as Kansas in August, and just as wholesome. If you're searching for family values, your search has ended. ⊠ *1149 E. Southern Ave., Mesa,* ☎ *602/813–5700. No credit cards.*

Mexican

$ ✕ **Rosa's Mexican Grill.** This festive, family-friendly restaurant summons up images of a Baja beach "taqueria" without the flies. The tacos are Rosa's true glory: beef, pork, and chicken are marinated in fruit juices and herbs for 12 hours, slowly oven-baked for another 10, then shredded and charbroiled. The fish taco, pepped up with cabbage, radishes, and lime, is also in a class by itself. Spoon on one of Rosa's five fresh homemade salsas. But beware the fiery habanero model —it can strip the enamel right off your teeth. ⊠ *328 E. University Dr., Mesa,* ☎ *602/964–5451. No credit cards. Closed Sun. and Mon.*

Middle Eastern

$ ✕ **Tasty Kabob.** Persian food is heavily seasoned, but never
★ spicy hot. Perfumed basmati rice, for example, is often teamed with several grilled kabobs—skewers of ground beef, lamb, chicken, or beef tenderloin. The stews here, called *khoresht* and *polo,* also give you a taste of authentic Persian fare. If *baghali polo* is on the menu, don't hesitate— it's dill-infused rice tossed with lima beans and lamb shank. ⊠ *1250 E. Apache Blvd., Tempe,* ☎ *602/966–0260. AE, D, MC, V. Closed Mon.*

West Valley: West Phoenix, Glendale, Litchfield Park

Asian

$–$$ ✕ **Big Wong.** Forget about Big Wong's hardbound menu and ask for the dog-eared, stapled sheets titled "Authentic Chinese Menu." Here you'll find the specialties that other Chinese restaurant chefs come to enjoy. Try the crabmeat and asparagus soup instead of wonton, or the broth made with shark's fin and shredded chicken. Bored with egg rolls? Try appetizers like smoked pork leg, deep-fried oysters, or cold jellyfish. Shrimp with vermicelli is one of the more unthreatening versions of clay-pot cooking, but risk takers may prefer the sea cucumber and duck-feet duo. ⊠ *616 W. Indian School Rd.,* ☎ *602/277–2870. MC, V. No lunch Sat.*

$–$$ ✕ **Pho Bang.** Tidy and unpretentious, Pho Bang delivers topnotch Vietnamese fare like catfish soup, an outstanding broth zipped up with lemon, pineapple, and fennel. Naturally there's *pho,* meal-size noodle soups stocked with various cuts of beef. Splurge on the shrimp and beef specialty and the server returns with three plates: one with transparently thin slices of marinated beef and raw shrimp; one with piles of mint, lettuce, cilantro, pickled leeks, cucumber, and carrot; and one with rice paper. Fire up the portable grill and cook the beef and shrimp. When they're done, combine with the veggies, roll in rice paper, and dip into the national condiment, fish sauce. It's all as good as it sounds. ⊠ *1702 W.*

Camelback Rd., ☎ *602/433–9440. Reservations not accepted. MC, V.*

International

$ ★ ✕ **Centro Cafe & Bakery.** If the word "value" makes you happy, this splendid restaurant will make you light up with pleasure. How the young chef-proprietor can deliver such big portions of powerfully flavored Mediterranean fare at such low prices is a question only his accountant can answer. In the meantime, savvy diners get to enjoy fresh-baked breads, pizzas, hearty pastas, chicken dishes, and homemade desserts. Everything sings with some combination of wine, garlic, lemon, capers, olives, sun-dried tomatoes, and cheese. Almost nothing on the menu goes for more than 10 bucks. ⊠ *15820 N. 35th Ave.,* ☎ *602/938–3383. AE, D, DC, MC, V. Closed Mon. No lunch weekends.*

$ ★ ✕ **Lalibela.** Locals are discovering that the Valley's only Ethiopian restaurant makes for a fun night out. Forget about silverware. Ethiopians wrap their food in *injera,* a spongy, slightly sour bread. Break off a piece and scoop up *doro wat,* chicken cooked in spiced butter sauce. *Alicha sega wat* brings beef bathed in a rich curry scented with turmeric. Vegetarian dishes are first-rate. True adventurers may opt for *kitfo,* finely ground raw beef mixed with butter and cardamom. ⊠ *849 W. University Dr., Tempe,* ☎ *602/829–1939. AE, D, MC, V. No lunch Mon.*

Mexican

$–$$ ✕ **Pepe's Taco Villa.** The neighborhood's not fancy, and neither is this restaurant. But in a town filled with gringoized, south-of-the-border fare, this is the real deal, an ethnic gem. Tacos rancheros, spicy, shredded pork pungently lathered with adobo paste, are a dream. So are the green corn tamales, *machacado* (air-dried beef), and chili relleno. But don't leave here without trying the sensational mole (pronounced *mo*-lay), a rich, exotic sauce fashioned from chilies and chocolate. ⊠ *2108 W. Camelback Rd.,* ☎ *602/242–0379. No credit cards. Closed Tues.*

$ ✕ **Las Cazuelas.** Set in a somewhat forlorn shopping strip, Las Cazuelas is bright and spiffy once you step in. Cheap, tasty, and family-friendly, it attracts locals yearning for fresh Mexican seafood. The Costa Brava is a seafood stew packed with shrimp, octopus, squid, clams, scallops, crab, and red snapper, accompanied by potatoes, carrots and squash in a lip-smacking broth fired with red chili. You'll get change back from a $10 bill, too. Landlubber dishes like the chili verde plate and carnitas burro are also quite tasty. ⊠ *5150 W. McDowell Rd.,* ☎ *602/278–4885. AE, DC, MC, V.*

$ ✕ **Lily's Cafe.** Friendly mom-and-pop proprietors, a jukebox with south-of-the-border hits, and low-priced fresh Mexican fare have kept patrons coming here for almost 50 years. Beef is the featured ingredient. The chimichanga (it's like a deep-fried burrito) is world-class, stuffed with tender beef and covered with cheese, guacamole, and sour cream. Fragrant tamales, spunky red chili beef, and chili rellenos right out of the fryer also shine. ⊠ *6706 N. 58th Dr., Glendale,* ☎ *602/937–7757. Reservations not accepted. No credit cards. Closed Mon. and Tues. and Aug.*

Southwestern

$$$– ✕ **Arizona Kitchen.** A few years ago, with the help of a re-
$$$$ searcher who studies Native American foods, management here put together a bold southwestern menu. Appetizers like blue corn piki rolls, stuffed with capon and goat cheese, and the wild boar anasazi bean chili give you an indication of what's to come. Entrées include grilled sirloin of buffalo in cabernet-and-vanilla chili negro sauce, and grilled venison medallions in blackberry zinfandel cocoa sauce. For dessert, try the chili-spiked ice cream in the striking turquoise "bowl" of hardened sugar. It's worth the 20-minute drive from downtown Phoenix. ⊠ *300 E. Indian School Rd. (Wigwam Resort), Litchfield Park,* ☎ *602/935–3811. AE, D, DC, MC, V. Closed Sun. and Mon. and July–Aug. No lunch.*

4 Lodging

F THERE'S ONE THING the Valley of the Sun knows how to do right, it's lodging, and metropolitan Phoenix has options ranging from world-class resorts to roadside motels, from upscale dude ranches to no-frills family-style operations where you can do your own cooking.

Most resorts are away from the heart of downtown Phoenix, though the renaissance of this area has brought new interest from hoteliers, with historic spots such as the Arizona Biltmore (still Phoenix's nicest) and the charming San Marcos being joined by many others. Most of the other resorts are in the neighboring, tourist-friendly city of Scottsdale, a destination in its own right; a few are scattered 20 to 30 mi to the north in the quickly expanding communities of Carefree and Cave Creek.

Most downtown Phoenix properties are business and family hotels, closer to the heart of the city—and to the average vacation budget. Many properties cater to corporate travelers during the week, but lower their weekend rates to entice leisure travelers; ask about weekend specials when making reservations.

Travelers flee snow and ice to bask in the Valley of the Sun. As a result, winter is the high season, peaking in January through March. Summer season—mid-May through the end of September—is giveaway time, when a night at one of the fanciest resorts often goes for a quarter of the winter price.

CATEGORY	COST*
$$$$	over $300
$$$	$200–$299
$$	$100–$199
$	under $100

All prices are for a standard double room during high season, excluding taxes and service charges.

Scottsdale

$$$$ **Hyatt Regency Scottsdale at Gainey Ranch.** A fun place for families, this resort has a huge water park with waterfalls, 10 pools, a water slide, lagoons plied by gondolas, and waterways that encircle three-quarters of the property. Three golf courses offer a choice of terrains—dunes, arroyo, or lakes—to suit a fancy for sand or water traps. The lobby is filled with stunning Native American sculpture and looks onto a large courtyard where weekend flamenco guitar performances are held. An innovative new project, the Hopi Center, provides exhibits and demonstrations, presided over by two Hopi Indians—it's a remarkable venture for a resort, and well worth a visit even for nonguests. Rooms are nicely sized and comfortable. ⊠ *7500 E. Doubletree Ranch Rd., Scottsdale 85258,* ☎ *602/991–3388 or 800/ 233–1234,* FAX *602/483–5550. 486 rooms, 7 casitas. 3 restaurants, bar, 10 pools, 3 9-hole golf courses, 8 tennis courts, croquet, health club, concierge floor, business services, free valet parking. AE, D, DC, MC, V.*

$$$$ ⊞ **Marriott's Camelback Inn.** Founded in the mid-1930s,
★ this historic resort is a swank oasis of comfort and relaxation in the gorgeous valley between Camelback and Mummy mountains, with the best-known spa in the area. The Camelback revels in its Southwest setting, from the stunning cacti adorning the 125-acre grounds to the latilla beam/kiva log lodgings. Rooms are notably spacious and varied in configuration—seven suites even have private swimming pools. A gallery displays Barry Goldwater's historic and landscape photographs, a revelation for those who didn't know of the former senator's talent with a camera. Visit the acclaimed spa, where you can indulge in a massage or in something more exotic like a Para-Joba Body Wrap or an Adobe Mud Purification Treatment. ⊠ *5402 E. Lincoln Dr., Scottsdale 85253,* ☎ *602/948–1700 or 800/ 242–2635,* FAX *602/951–8469. 420 rooms, 27 suites. 5 restaurants, lounge, coffee shop, 3 pools, spa, 2 18-hole golf courses, 6 tennis courts, hiking, business services, meeting rooms, free parking. AE, D, DC, MC, V.*

$$$$ ⊞ **The Phoenician.** Guests enter a bright, airy lobby to find
★ towering fountains, gleaming marble, and smiling faces of a service staff who will do handsprings to satisfy. French-provincial decor and authentic Dutch-master paintings are a bit of a surprise in the desert, creating a sumptuous atmosphere. A 2-acre cactus garden showcases hundreds of varieties of cacti and succulents, the Centre for Well Being spa has an inspiring meditation atrium, and the resort's cen-

Phoenix and Scottsdale Lodging

Hayden Rhodes Rd

Bell Rd.

Greenway Rd.

Thunderbird

Lookout
Mountain
Preserve

Cactus

Shea Blvd.

Dunlap Ave.

PARADISE
VALLEY

Squaw Peak

Lincoln Dr.

Glendale Ave.

Mc D

Bethany Home Rd.

Camelback

Heard Museum

Phoenix
Art Museum

McDowell Rd.

Red Mountain Fwy.

Van Buren St.

Papago Fwy.

Buckeye Rd.

Sky Harbor
International
Airport

Salt River

Southern Ave.

Baseline Rd.

South Mountain
Park

Black Canyon Fwy.

7th St.

7th Ave.

Central Ave.

7th St.

16th St.

19th Ave.

Squaw Peak Pkwy.

24th St.

32nd St.

32nd St.

40th St.

44th St.

Tatum Blvd.

Priest Dr.

48th St.

9th Ave.

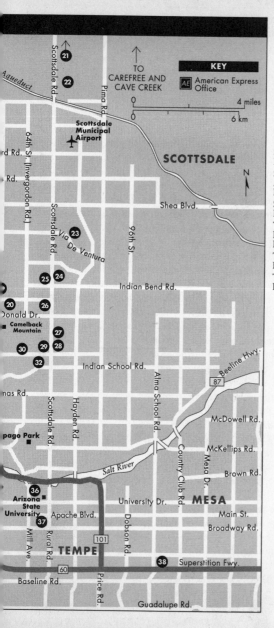

KEY

Ⓐ American Express Office

0   4 miles
0   6 km

TO
CAREFREE AND
CAVE CREEK

Aqueduct

Scottsdale Rd.

Pima Rd.

Scottsdale
Municipal
Airport

SCOTTSDALE

N

64th St. (Invergordon Rd.)

rd Rd.

Rd.

Scottsdale Rd.

Via De Ventura

96th St.

Shea Blvd.

Indian Bend Rd.

Donald Dr.

Camelback
Mountain

Indian School Rd.

Alma School Rd.

Beeline Hwy.

87

McDowell Rd.

Hayden Rd.

Scottsdale Rd.

nas Rd.

pago Park

Salt River

Country Club Rd.

Mesa Dr.

McKellips Rd.

Brown Rd.

Arizona
State
University

University Dr.

Apache Blvd.

MESA

Main St.

Broadway Rd.

Mill Ave.

Rural Rd.

101

TEMPE

Dobson Rd.

Price Rd.

38

Superstition Fwy.

60

Baseline Rd.

Guadalupe Rd.

21

22

23

25   24

20

26

27

30   29   28

32

36

37

terpiece pool is lined with mother-of-pearl tiles. Rooms are
spacious, with cream walls, tasteful rattan furnishings in
muted tones, Italian marble bathrooms, and private patios.
Ask for a room facing south, with views of the resort's pools
and the city. In a city known for great dining, the Phoenician can lay claim to three of the area's finest restaurants,
Mary Elaine's, the Terrace Dining Room (☞ Chapter 3),
and Windows on the Green. ⊠ *6000 E. Camelback Rd.,
Scottsdale 85251, ☎ 602/941–8200 or 800/888–8234. 581
rooms, 73 suites. 4 restaurants, 9 pools, barbershop, beauty
salon, sauna, steam room, golf privileges, 12 tennis courts,
archery, badminton, basketball, croquet, health club, jogging, volleyball, pro shop, billiards, children's programs,
business services, free parking. AE, D, DC, MC, V.*

\$\$\$\$ 🏨 **Scottsdale Princess.** On the 450 beautifully landscaped
acres of this resort, Mexican-colonial architecture is set
against the splendor of the McDowell Mountains. Built
around a series of outdoor areas, the resort has a wonder-
fully open feel. Rooms in the red-tile-roof main building
and the casitas are furnished in desert-sand tones with pink
accents, and the resort's emphasis on spaciousness is echoed
in details like "walk-around" tile showers and immense closets. The Marquesa restaurant (☞ Chapter 3) has been con-
sistently rated one of the best in the state. The landscape
director leads tours of the grounds, which are lush with
palms, bougainvillea, and rosemary shrubs (each restaurant
has its own herb garden). For perfect sunset-gazing, choose
the quiet east pool, where the distant mountains are perfectly framed by a circle of palms. ⊠ *7575 E. Princess Dr.,
Scottsdale 85255, ☎ 602/585–4848 or 800/344–4758, ℻
602/585–0091. 429 rooms, 21 suites, 125 casitas, 75 villas. 5 restaurants, bar, 3 pools, spa, steam room, 2 18-hole
golf courses, 7 tennis courts, health club, racquetball,
squash, pro shops, business services, free parking. AE, D,
DC, MC, V.*

\$\$\$– 🏨 **Scottsdale Plaza Resort.** Arched doorways, soft-beige
\$\$\$\$ stucco, and tiered stone fountains lend Old World charm
to this hotel's Spanish-Mediterranean feel. Although it
lacks the requisite lush golf fairways, this 40-acre independent hotel is out to compete with the five-star big boys.
Special-touch amenities—such as the box of chocolate truf-
fles left on the pillow—accompany more pragmatic luxu-

ries like 2-ft-thick walls between rooms. Suites are arranged around a courtyard pool, and the resort boasts Arizona's largest hot tub. The lounge at Remington's, the hotel's main restaurant, features jazz combos. ⊠ *7200 N. Scottsdale Rd., Scottsdale 85253,* ☎ *602/948–5000 or 800/832–2025,* FAX *602/951–5152. 224 rooms, 170 suites, 20 lodges. 2 restaurants, 3 lounges, 5 pools, beauty salon, 3 outdoor spas, putting green, 5 tennis courts, exercise room, 3 racquetball courts, pro shop, free parking. AE, D, DC, MC, V.*

$$$ ▥ **Marriott's Mountain Shadows.** Across the street from the more upscale Camelback Inn, this Marriott property is a ranch-style resort, perfect for families and enviably located, as its name implies, right at the base of Camelback Mountain. Although the furnishings aren't as distinctive as at its high-class sister property, rooms are large and comfortable, with walk-in closets and spacious sitting areas. Creeks and a waterfall make the highly regarded golf course a duffer's oasis; you can even play night golf, complete with glow-in-the-dark balls. ⊠ *5641 E. Lincoln Dr., Scottsdale 85253,* ☎ *602/948–7111 or 800/228–9200,* FAX *602/951–5430. 318 rooms, 19 suites. 3 restaurants, lounge, 3 pools, 2 hydrotherapy pools, massage, sauna, 18-hole executive golf course, putting green, 8 lighted tennis courts, exercise room, Ping Pong, pro shops, meeting facilities, airport limo service, complimentary valet parking. AE, D, DC, MC, V.*

$$$ ▥ **Radisson Resort Scottsdale.** With myriad sports options, this hotel is the perfect match for active types who desire the facilities of a swank resort in a low-key setting. Two-story buildings house guest rooms, accessible via pathways winding through the well-kept grounds. The large, airy lobby has brick columns, white ceilings, and massive fountains. The spacious rooms are done in teal and peach tones, with patios or balconies, big closets, and sitting areas. Be sure to spend an evening in Tapps, the resort's pub, which features 12 specialty beers on draft. ⊠ *7171 N. Scottsdale Rd., Scottsdale 85253, 602/991–3800 or 800/333–3333,* FAX *602/948–1381. 284 rooms, 32 bi-level suites, 2 luxury suites. Restaurant, 2 bars, patisserie, 3 pools, beauty salon, spa, 2 18-hole golf courses, 21 tennis courts, volleyball. AE, D, DC, MC, V.*

$$$ ⚏ **Renaissance Cottonwoods Resort.** Shopaholics will like this 25-acre resort—it's across the street from the shops and restaurants of Scottsdale's Borgata Shopping Center (☞ Chapter 7). Check in among pottery and large cacti in the low-key, salmon-color lobby; you'll be chauffeured in a golf cart to your room in one of the adobe buildings. White stucco rooms are pleasant, with light wood furniture, beamed ceilings, and small but well-kept bathrooms. The suites are much grander, boasting private hot tubs, large living rooms, and minibars. ⊠ *6100 N. Scottsdale Rd., Scottsdale 85253,* ☎ *602/991–1414,* 𝖥𝖠𝖷 *602/951–3350. 64 rooms, 107 villas. Restaurant, 2 pools, 4 tennis courts, meeting facilities. AE, D, DC, MC, V.*

$$$ ⚏ **Sunburst Resort.** This sedate, low-rise hotel may be Scottsdale's best-kept secret. Five two-story structures line grounds dotted with orange trees and Adirondack chairs clustered beneath oversized canvas umbrellas. Roomy accommodations are decorated with patterned bedspreads in vivid, primary colors, benches upholstered in whimsical cow-print material, and intricately carved pine furnishings; French doors open onto private balconies. Motorists will appreciate parking close to the room. ⊠ *4925 N. Scottsdale Rd., Scottsdale 85251,* ☎ *602/945–7666. 205 rooms, 5 suites. Restaurant, bar, pool, refrigerators, exercise room, meeting rooms, free parking. AE, D, DC, MC, V.*

$$ ⚏ **Safari Resort.** Built in the 1940s, the Safari was one of the city's first resorts and still exudes a kitsch appeal. The lobby has a mirrored ceiling, huge turquoise lamps, and end tables that look like giant boulders; near the reception desk is a squawking parrot in a cage. Two stories of "Palm-Beach–style" rooms have sliding Arcadia-door entrances and private patios or balconies that overlook lawns flanked with magnolia trees and swaying palms. The Safari's not posh; in fact, as a "resort," it's rather downscale, but plentiful amenities at affordable prices—travelers love the free local phone calls and free-flowing coffee in the lobby—might win over the unfussy. ⊠ *4611 N. Scottsdale Rd., Scottsdale 85251,* ☎ *602/945–0721 or 800/845–4356,* 𝖥𝖠𝖷 *602/946–4703. 178 rooms, 10 suites. Restaurant, bar, coffee shop, refrigerators, 2 pools, beauty salon, putting green, horseshoes, shuffleboard, volleyball, coin laundry, free parking. AE, D, MC, V.*

$ ☷ Motel 6 Scottsdale. The best bargain in Scottsdale lodging is easy to miss, but it's worth hunting for as it's close to the specialty shops of 5th Avenue and Scottsdale's Civic Plaza. Amenities aren't a priority here, but the price is remarkable considering the stylish and much more expensive resorts found close by. Rooms are small and spare with blue carpets, print bedspreads, and a small desk and wardrobe. And how many Motel 6 properties have a pool surrounded by palms and rooms with a view of Camelback Mountain? ☒ *6848 E. Camelback Rd., Scottsdale 85251, ☎ 602/946–2280 or 800/466–8356, ℻ 602/949–7583. 122 rooms. Pool, hot tub, parking. AE, D, DC, MC, V.*

$ ☷ Scottsdale's 5th Avenue Inn. The most attractive feature of this three-story, exterior corridor motel is its walking distance to Scottsdale's Old Town and boutique/gallery enclave. Modest rooms have standard but serviceable furnishings that include a sofa, coffee table, and petite writing desk, as well as a large open-closet dressing area. Don't come expecting luxury; what you will find is a friendly welcome and a blessedly short stroll to some of the area's finest shopping—which in this city based on the almighty auto is a rarity. ☒ *6935 Fifth Ave., Scottsdale 85251, ☎ 602/994–9461 or 800/528–7396, ℻ 602/947–1695. 92 rooms. Breakfast room, pool, hot tub, free parking. AE, D, DC, MC, V.*

North of Scottsdale: Carefree and Cave Creek

$$$$ ☷ The Boulders. The Valley's most serene and secluded lux-
★   ury resort hides among hill-size, 12-million-year-old granite boulders in the foothills town of Carefree, just over the border from Scottsdale. Casitas snuggled into the rocks have exposed log-beam ceilings, ceiling fans, and curved, pueblo-style half-walls and shelves. Each has a patio with a view, a miniature kiva fireplace, and spacious bathrooms with deep tubs. Luxury touches abound, from champagne upon arrival to "couples massages" available in the privacy of your casita. Boutiques and a satellite branch of the Heard Museum are on the property, and golfers stay here to play on two premier courses. ☒ *34631 N. Tom Darlington Dr., Carefree 85377, ☎ 602/488–9009 or 800/553–1717, ℻ 602/488–4118. 160 casitas, 33 patio homes. 4 restaurants, 2 pools, spa, 2 18-hole golf courses, 6 tennis courts,*

exercise room, hiking, horseback riding, jogging, business services, meeting rooms, free parking. AE, D, DC, MC, V.

North Central Phoenix: Biltmore District

$$$$ ⚅ **Arizona Biltmore.** Designed by Frank Lloyd Wright's col-
★ league Albert Chase McArthur, the Biltmore has remained
the premier resort in central Phoenix since it opened in 1929.
The dramatic lobby, with its stained-glass skylights, wrought-
iron pilasters, and cozy sitting alcoves, fills with piano
music in the evenings, inviting guests to linger. Impeccably
manicured grounds have open walkways, fountains, and
flower beds in colorful bloom. Story has it that the Catalina
Pool's blue and gold tiles so enchanted former owner
William Wrigley, Jr., that he bought the factory that produced them. Rooms have marble bathrooms and the same
low-key elegance as the rest of the hotel, decorated in earth
tones and accented with southwestern-patterned acces-
sories. You'll be in good company: various celebrities—and
every American president since Herbert Hoover—have
stayed here. ⊠ *24th St. and Missouri Ave., Phoenix 85016,*
☎ *602/955–6600 or 800/950–0086,* 🖷 *602/381–7600.*
600 rooms, 50 villas. 3 restaurants, lobby lounge, 6 pools,
2 18-hole golf courses, putting green, 8 tennis courts, health
club, jogging, concierge, car rental, free parking. AE, D,
DC, MC, V.

$$$ ⚅ **Embassy Suites Biltmore.** Across the street from Biltmore
Fashion Park, this large all-suites hotel has a cheery, informal
feel. Huge palms, boulders, and waterfalls punctuate an airy
lobby, and mazelike paths lead to lodgings around the
atrium. The pleasant suites have small living rooms, larger
bedrooms, wet bars, and nicely appointed baths. Compli-
mentary breakfast and afternoon cocktails are thoughtful
perks. ⊠ *2630 E. Camelback Rd., Phoenix 85016,* ☎ *602/*
955–3992 or 800/362–2779, 🖷 *602/955–3992. 232*
suites. Restaurant, lounge, pool, fitness room, hot tub. AE,
D, DC, MC, V.

$$$ ⚅ **Ritz-Carlton.** This sand-color neo-Federal facade facing
Biltmore Fashion Park hides a graceful, well-appointed
luxury hotel. Large public rooms decorated with 18th- and
19th-century European paintings house a handsome china
collection. Rooms, done in shades of ice blue and peach,

have stocked refrigerators, irons with ironing boards, feather and foam pillows, safes, armoires that contain TVs, and white-marble bath basins. Choose between mountain or city vistas. ⊠ *2401 E. Camelback Rd., Phoenix 85016,* ☎ *602/468–0700 or 800/241–3333,* FAX *602/468–0793. 281 rooms, 14 suites. Restaurant, 2 bars, pool, 2 saunas, tennis court, exercise room, bicycles, concierge floor, business services, parking (fee). AE, D, DC, MC, V.*

$$ 🏨 **Camelback Courtyard by Marriott.** Built in 1990, this four-story hostelry delivers compact elegance in its public areas (lots of plants, white tile, and wood) and reliable, no-frills comfort in its rooms and suites. A lap pool and Jacuzzi await in the landscaped courtyard. More than 50 restaurants are within walking distance. ⊠ *2101 E. Camelback Rd., Phoenix 85016,* ☎ *602/955–5200,* FAX *602/955–1101. 144 rooms, 11 suites. Breakfast room, bar, room service, pool, hot tub, exercise room, meeting rooms, free parking. AE, D, DC, MC, V.*

$$ 🏨 **Phoenix Inn.** A block off a popular stretch of Camelback Road, this three-story property is a remarkable bargain, considering it has amenities not generally seen in properties of the same price category—leather love seats, refrigerators, coffeemakers, hair dryers, and microwaves. Several rooms have corner Jacuzzis. Continental breakfast is served daily from 6 to 10, in a pleasant breakfast room with a large television. ⊠ *2310 E. Highland Ave., Phoenix 85016,* ☎ *602/ 956–5221 or 800/956–5221,* FAX *602/468–7220. 114 rooms, 6 suites. Breakfast room, pool, hot tub, exercise room, gift shop, coin laundry. AE, D, DC, MC, V.*

Northeast Phoenix and Paradise Valley

$$$$ 🏨 **Royal Palms.** Once the home of Cunard Steamship executive Delos T. Cooke, the Royal Palms was a rather forgettable property until its 1997 overhaul. This Mediterranean-style resort has beautifully maintained courtyards with antique fountains, a stately row of the namesake palms at its entrance, and individually designed, stylish rooms. The deluxe casitas are each done in a different theme—Trompe l'Oeil, Romantic Retreat, Spanish Colonial—by members of the American Society of Interior Designers. The restaurant, T. Cook's, is one of the most

popular in town. ⊠ *5200 E. Camelback Rd., Phoenix, 85018,* ☎ *602/840–3610 or 800/672–6011,* 𝔽𝔸𝕏 *602/840–6927. 112 rooms and casitas, 4 suites. Restaurant, bar, pool, tennis court, fitness center, business services, meeting rooms, free valet parking. AE, D, DC, MC, V.*

$$$–
$$$$
★   🏨 **Hermosa Inn.** The ranch-style lodge at the heart of this small resort was the home and studio of cowboy artist Lon Megargee in the 1930s; today the adobe structure houses Lon's (☞ Chapter 3), justly popular for its New American cuisine and amiable staff. The inn, on 6 acres of lush lawn mixed with desert landscaping, is a hidden jewel of hospitality and low-key luxury. Villas as big as private homes and individually decorated casitas hold an enviable collection of art. The secluded Garden Court's hot tub is set in a beautifully designed courtyard. A blessedly peaceful alternative to some of the larger resorts, the Hermosa offers serenity, attention to detail, and alluring accommodations. ⊠ *5532 N. Palo Cristi Rd., Paradise Valley 85253,* ☎ *602/955–8614 or 800/241–1210,* 𝔽𝔸𝕏 *602/955–8299. 4 villas, 3 haciendas, 22 casitas, 17 ranchos. Restaurant, bar, kitchenettes, pool, 2 hot tubs, 3 tennis courts, free parking. Full breakfast. AE, D, DC, MC, V.*

$$$ 🏨 **Doubletree La Posada Resort.** Camelback Mountain provides a spectacular backdrop for this sprawling resort with extensive athletic and sports facilities. The vast Lagoon Pool is the resort's centerpiece, replete with cascading waterfalls, passageways under red boulder formations, and the Grotto Bar. Large rooms sport iron furniture and Navajo-patterned bedspreads; all have patios, data ports, and bathrooms with double vanities. The property's tile floors, mauve/maroon carpets, and amusing chandeliers might make you think you're in a time warp (the place was built in 1978), and the lounge's round, sunken disco floor may fulfill your burning, unresolved "Saturday Night Fever" fantasies. ⊠ *4949 E. Lincoln Dr., Paradise Valley 85253,* ☎ *602/952–0420 or 800/222–8733,* 𝔽𝔸𝕏 *602/840–8576. 252 rooms, 10 suites. Restaurant, lounge, 2 pools, 4 hot tubs, beauty salon, massage, sauna, 2 putting greens, 6 tennis courts, exercise room, horseshoes, racquetball, volleyball, pro shop, nightclub, free parking. AE, D, DC, MC, V.*

$$ 🏨 **La Estancia Bed and Breakfast Inn.** A rare find in this
★   valley of megaresorts: a five-room bed-and-breakfast offering

creature comforts, personal attention, and a perfect Camelback Road location. Particularly appealing is the Southwest Room, with leather and wood furniture, iron light fixtures, and salmon-and-black–tiled bathroom. The frillier Mountain View Room—a honeymoon suite—has a wrought-iron, king-size four poster bed, pastel walls, and balcony overlooking Camelback. There's a spacious parlor and lovely patio where you can enjoy breakfast—try the French toast stuffed with cinnamon/walnut cream cheese—under lemon trees. A cape honeysuckle, popular with hummingbirds, shades the tiny pool, and the grounds are luxuriant with hibiscus, roses, orchid trees, and citrus trees which guests are welcome to harvest. ⊠ *4797 E. Camelback Rd., Phoenix 85018,* ☎ *602/808–9924 or 800/410–7655,* FAX *602/808–9925. 5 rooms. In-room hot tubs, pool. Full breakfast. AE, D, DC, MC, V.*

Central Phoenix

$$$– ⊞ **Hilton Suites.** This practical and popular 11-story atrium
$$$$ is a model of excellent design within tight limits. It sits off Central Avenue, 2 mi north of downtown amid the "Central Corridor" cluster of office towers. The marble-floor, pillared lobby opens into an atrium containing palm trees, natural boulder fountains, glass elevators, and a lantern-lighted café, where guests enjoy a bite. Each room has an exercise bike and VCR, and a large walk-through bathroom between the living room and bedroom. ⊠ *10 E. Thomas Rd., Phoenix 85012,* ☎ *602/222–1111 or 800/445–8667,* FAX *602/265–4841. 226 suites. Restaurant, bar, kitchenettes, refrigerators, in-room VCRs, indoor lap pool, sauna, hot tub, exercise room, free parking. AE, D, DC, MC, V.*

$$$ ⊞ **Hyatt Regency Phoenix.** The real draw of this hotel is its revolving restaurant with its panoramic views of the Phoenix area. The hotel itself is best left to conventioneers; leisure travelers will likely be put off by the factory-like atmosphere and the dourness of the hotel staff. The spare, seven-story, all-white atrium—there's a surreal, space-station feel here—is punctuated by huge sculptures and whooshing glass elevators. It all manages to be impressive without quite being attractive, though rooms are spacious and comfortable. Note: The atrium roof blocks east views on floors 8 to 10. ✉ *122 N. 2nd St., Phoenix 85004,* ☎ *602/252–1234,* FAX *602/254–9472. 667 rooms. 45 suites. 2 restaurants, bar, pool, exercise rooms, concierge, business services, meeting rooms, car rental. AE, D, DC, MC, V.*

$$–$$$ 🏨 **Embassy Suites Phoenix Airport West.** Just minutes from downtown, this four-story courtyard hotel has lush palms and olive trees surrounding bubbling fountains and a sunken pool. Complimentary breakfast, cooked to order, and an evening social hour are offered in the spacious atrium lounge. Rooms have hair dryers, irons and ironing boards, and wet bars with microwaves, sinks, and mini-refrigerator. ✉ *2333 E. Thomas Rd., Phoenix 85016,* ☎ *602/ 957–1910,* FAX *602/955–2861. 183 suites. Restaurant, kitchenettes, refrigerators, pool, hot tub, exercise room, laundry service, airport shuttle, free parking. Full breakfast. AE, D, DC, MC, V.*

$$ 🏨 **Hotel San Carlos.** Built in 1927, this seven-story hotel is a step back in time: classical music, wall tapestries, Austrian crystal chandeliers, shiny copper elevators—you'll ride Phoenix's first to your room—and an accommodating staff transport you to a more genteel era. Among other distinctions, the San Carlos was the area's first air-conditioned hotel—its sign used to boast "Air Cooled"—and suites bear the names of movie star guests like Marilyn Monroe and Spencer Tracy. Rooms, rather snug by modern standards, have attractive period furnishings, including marble-topped desks and wood armoires (and if you think the rooms are small, wait until you see the pool). Upgrading of room amenities and restoration of the lobby's original marble floors are in progress. ✉ *202 N. Central Ave., Phoenix 85004,* ☎ *602/253–4121 or 800/528–5446,* FAX *602/253–6668. 132 rooms. Restaurant, café, pool, exercise room, meeting rooms, parking (fee). AE, D, DC, MC, V.*

$$ 🏨 **Lexington Hotel.** Phoenix's best bet for fitness enthusiasts and sports-lovers, the Lexington houses a 45,000-square-ft health facility, which includes, among other things, a full-size indoor basketball court, a 40-station machine workout center, and a large outdoor waterfall pool. The ambience is bright, modern, and informal. Rooms range in size from moderate (in the cabana wing, first-floor rooms have poolside patios) to very small (tower wing). This is where visiting teams—and fans—like to stay. ✉ *100 W.*

Clarendon Ave., Phoenix 85013, ☎ *602/279–9811,* ℻ *602/ 285–2932. 180 rooms. Sports bar, pool, beauty salon, hot tub, massage, sauna, steam room, health club, basketball, racquetball, free parking. AE, D, DC, MC, V.*

$–$$ 🏨 **Quality Hotel & Resort.** With a 1.5-acre Getaway Lagoon ringed by exotic palms and bamboo, the Quality is central Phoenix's best bargain oasis. Rooms and public areas are simply furnished, and the newly opened VIP floor offers cabana suites and a private rooftop pool with views of downtown Phoenix's ever-changing skyline. ⊠ *3600 N. 2nd Ave., Phoenix 85013,* ☎ *602/248–0222 or 800/256–1237,* ℻ *602/265–6331. 257 rooms, 23 suites. Restaurant, bar, 4 pools, hot tub, putting green, basketball, exercise room, shuffleboard, volleyball, outdoor theater, playground, laundry, business center, free covered parking. AE, D, DC, MC, V.*

North and West Phoenix

$$$$ 🏨 **Wigwam Resort.** Built in 1918 as a retreat for executives of the Goodyear Company, the Wigwam has the pleasing feel of an upscale lodge. You'll still find a wealth of perks, primary among them two top-notch designer golf courses. Casita-style rooms, situated along paths overflowing with cacti, palms, and huge bougainvillea, are decorated in a tasteful southwestern style: distressed-wood furniture, iron lamps, pastel walls, and brightly patterned spreads. Local artwork adorns the walls and all rooms have patios. The business center is in a separate wing so as to not mix business with pleasure, and the immense suites have parlors that can hold up to 300 of your closest friends. It's easy to see how this isolated world of graciousness inspires a fierce loyalty in its guests, some of whom have been returning for more than 50 years. ⊠ *300 Wigwam Blvd., Litchfield Park 85340,* ☎ *602/935–3811 or 800/327–0396,* ℻ *602/935–3737. 261 rooms, 70 suites. 3 restaurants, 3 bars, 2 pools, 2 hot tubs, beauty salon, 3 18-hole golf courses, 9 tennis courts, basketball, croquet, exercise room, Ping Pong, shuffleboard, volleyball, pro shop, children's programs, business services, meeting room, free parking. AE, D, DC, MC, V.*

$$$– 🏨 **Pointe Hilton at Squaw Peak.** The most family-oriented
$$$$ of the Pointe group, Squaw Peak features a 9-acre recreation area known as the Hole-in-the-Wall River Ranch

with swimming pools fed by man-made waterfalls, a 130-ft water slide, and a 1,000-ft "river" that winds past mini-golf course, tennis courts, outdoor decks, and artificial buttes with stunning mountain vistas. The Coyote Camp keeps kids busy with activities from gold panning to arts and crafts. Accommodations in the pink stucco buildings vary in size from standard two-room suites to the grand three-bedroom Palacio; all have two or more televisions, wet bars, and balconies. Families prefer the bi-level suites. ⊠ *7877 N. 16th St., Phoenix 85020,* ☎ *602/997–2626 or 800/876–4683,* ℻ *602/997–2391. 431 suites, 130 casitas, 1 3-bedroom house. 3 restaurants, 3 lounges, 7 pools, 18-hole golf course, miniature golf, spa, 4 tennis courts, exercise room, hiking, Ping Pong, water volleyball and basketball, mountain bikes, shops, children's programs, meeting rooms. AE, D, DC, MC, V.*

$$$–
$$$$
🖭 **The Pointe Hilton at Tapatio Cliffs.** This oasis, snuggled into 400 acres at the base of Phoenix North Mountain Desert Park, has some of the Valley's most spectacular views. The lobby has an open, airy feel, with beamed chalet-type ceilings, so the bright purple carpeting and bold bedspreads in the rooms come as something of a surprise. But the whitewashed wood furniture, tin mirrors, marble counters, and well-chosen art are all nice touches. The resort's centerpiece is "The Falls," an award-winning 3-acre creation unveiled in 1997: a 40-ft cascade fed by mountain waterfalls ends in 12 travertine pools, surrounded by tiled terraces and flower gardens. The on-site restaurant, Different Pointe of View, is a perennial favorite for its regional American cuisine and fabulous view. ⊠ *11111 N. 7th St., Phoenix 85020,* ☎ *602/866–7500 or 800/876–4683,* ℻ *602/993–0276. 584 suites. 3 restaurants, 3 lounges, 7 swimming pools, spa, 18-hole golf course, 11 tennis courts, exercise room, hiking, horseback riding, jogging, mountain bikes, business services, meeting rooms, hourly airport transportation. AE, D, DC, MC, V.*

Near Sky Harbor Airport

$$$–
$$$$
🖭 **Pointe Hilton on South Mountain.** The Southwest's largest resort, 15 minutes from downtown, sits next to South Mountain Park, a 16,000-acre desert preserve. Rooms and

public areas are serviceable, but the facilities are the real draw: the Pointe offers a premier four-story sports center, four restaurants, and various outdoor activities, from golf and tennis to horseback riding and mountain biking. Landscaped walkways and roads link everything on the 750-acre property; carts and drivers are always on call. ✉ 7777 S. Pointe Pkwy., Phoenix 85044, ☎ 602/438–9000 or 800/876–4683, FAX 602/431–6535. 638 suites. 4 restaurants, 6 pools, saunas, 18-hole golf course, 10 tennis courts, health club, hiking, horseback riding, jogging, racquetball, volleyball, mountain bikes, pro shop, coin laundry, meeting rooms, free parking. AE, D, DC, MC, V.

$$$ 🏨 **The Buttes.** Two miles east of Sky Harbor, nestled in desert buttes at I–10 and AZ 60, this hotel joins dramatic architecture (the lobby's back wall is the volcanic rock itself) and classic Southwest design (pine and saguaro-rib furniture, works by major regional artists) with stunning Valley views. "Radial" rooms are largest, with the widest views; inside rooms face the huge free-form pools, with waterfall, hot tubs, and poolside cantina. The elegant Top of the Rock restaurant is a definite plus. ✉ 2000 Westcourt Way, Tempe 85282, ☎ 602/225–9000 or 800/843–1986, FAX 602/438–8622. 353 rooms. 2 restaurants, 3 bars, 2 pools, 4 hot tubs, sauna, 4 tennis courts, exercise room, hiking, jogging, bicycles, shop, concierge floor, business services, meeting rooms, free parking. AE, D, DC, MC, V.

$$ 🏨 **Doubletree Guest Suites.** In the Gateway Center, just 1½ mi north of the airport, this honeycomb of six-story towers is the best of a dozen choices for the traveler who wants to get off the plane and into a comfortable, centrally located property. Rooms have wet bars with microwaves and refrigerators. Vacationers beware: bedroom furnishings cater to corporate guests traveling light—two-drawer credenzas serve as bureaus and dinky wardrobes function as closets. ✉ 320 N. 44th St., Phoenix 85008, ☎ 602/225–0500 or 800/800–3098, FAX 602/225–0957. 242 suites. Restaurant, bar, pool, sauna, exercise room, meeting rooms, free parking. AE, D, DC, MC, V.

$$ 🏨 **Hampton Inn Airport.** This four-story, interior-corridor hotel 9 mi from downtown is both affordable and accommodating. Rooms are moderate size, appointed with handsome armoires and bright-colored leaf or fish prints for drapes and bedspreads. Free Continental breakfast is available in the lobby, where a good-size television is tuned to the local wake-up news show. Take advantage of the hotel shuttle running from 5 AM to midnight. ⊠ *4234 S. 48th St., Phoenix 85040,* ☎ *602/438–8688 or 800-426-7876,* FAX *602/431–8339. 130 rooms, 4 suites. In-room VCRs, pool, hot tub, jogging, meeting rooms, airport shuttle, free parking. Continental breakfast. AE, D, DC, MC, V.*

East Valley: Tempe and Mesa

$$ 🏨 **Hilton Pavilion.** This sand-and-rose-color eight-story hotel has a southwestern look. Rooms are medium size, with plum and teal carpeting, average-size baths, small closets, and a large lighted table; corner suites and the top two floors have the best views. The hotel is in the heart of the East Valley, just off AZ 60, and the immense Fiesta Mall is across the street; downtown Phoenix is 18 mi away. ⊠ *1011 W. Holmes Ave., Mesa 85210,* ☎ *602/833–5555 or 800/ 544–5866,* FAX *602/649–1380. 201 rooms, 62 suites. Restaurant, 2 bars, refrigerators, pool, hot tub, exercise room, business services, free parking. AE, D, DC, MC, V.*

$$ 🏨 **Tempe Mission Palms Hotel.** Set between the Arizona State University campus and Old Town Tempe, this three-story courtyard hotel is handy to the East Valley and downtown Phoenix. The tone is set by a handsome, casual lobby—Matisse-inspired upholstery on overstuffed chairs—and an energetic young staff. Many visitors stay here for ASU sports and pro-football Cardinals events (the stadium is virtually next door). Rooms are bright, simple southwestern, and comfortable. The hotel's popular "Monster Bar"—adorned with an 8-ft-long Gila monster suspended from the ceiling—becomes a lively sports lounge at game time. ⊠ *60 E. 5th St., Tempe 85281,* ☎ *602/894–1400 or 800/547–8705,* FAX *602/968–7677. 303 rooms. Restaurant, bar, pool, sauna, 3 tennis courts, exercise room, business services, meeting rooms, airport shuttle, free parking. AE, D, DC, MC, V.*

$$ 🏨 **Twin Palms Hotel.** Across the street from ASU's Gammage Auditorium and minutes from Old Town Tempe, this seven-story high-rise hotel has a domed-window facade. Faux finishes creatively mask dated, textured walls in the rooms, and corner basins strike strategic blows to cramped bathrooms. Guests receive free admission to facilities at the nearby ASU Recreation Complex with three Olympic-size pools, badminton and squash courts, and aerobics classes. ✉ *225 E. Apache Blvd., Tempe 85281,* ☎ *602/967–9431 or 800/367–0835,* ℻ *602/303–6602. 140 rooms, 1 suite. Bar, pool, concierge floor, airport shuttle, free parking. AE, DC, MC, V.*

5 Nightlife and the Arts

THE ARTS

Phoenix performing-arts groups have grown rapidly in number and sophistication, especially over the past two decades. The **Herberger Theater Center** (⊠ 222 E. Monroe St., ☎ 602/252–8497) is the permanent home to the Arizona Theatre Company, Actors Theatre of Phoenix, and Ballet Arizona, and also presents visiting dance troupes and orchestras.

Facing the Herberger Theater, **Symphony Hall** (⊠ 225 E. Adams St., ☎ 602/262–7272) is home to the Phoenix Symphony and Arizona Opera as well as a venue for pop concerts by top-name performers. The **Orpheum Theatre** (⊠ 203 W. Adams St., ☎ 602/252–9678) showcases various performing arts, including children's theater, and film festivals. Arizona State University splits an impressive performance schedule between the **Gammage Auditorium** (⊠ Mill Ave. at Apache Blvd., Tempe, ☎ 602/965–3434), **Sundome Center** (⊠ 19403 R. H. Johnson Blvd., Sun City West, ☎ 602/975–1900), and **Kerr Cultural Center** (⊠ 6110 N. Scottsdale Rd., Scottsdale, ☎ 602/965–5377).

The most comprehensive ticket agencies are the **Arizona State University Public Events Box Office** (⊠ Gammage Center, Tempe, ☎ 602/965–3434) and **Dillard's ticket line** (☎ 602/503–5555 or 800/638–4253).

Classical Music

Arizona Opera (⊠ 4600 N. 12th St., Phoenix, ☎ 602/266–7464), one of the nation's most respected regional companies, stages an opera season, primarily classical, in Tucson and Phoenix. The Phoenix season runs October to March at Symphony Hall.

Phoenix Symphony Orchestra (⊠ 455 N. 3rd St., Suite 390, Phoenix, ☎ 602/495–1999), the resident company at Symphony Hall, has reached the first rank of American regional symphonies. Its rich season includes orchestral works from classical and contemporary literature, a chamber series, composer festivals, and outdoor pops concerts.

Dance

A. Ludwig Co. (☎ 602/965–3914), the Valley's foremost modern dance troupe, includes choreography by founder-director Ann Ludwig, an ASU faculty member, in its repertoire of contemporary works.

Ballet Arizona (✉ 3645 E. Indian School Rd., ☎ 602/381–1096), the state's professional ballet company, presents a full season of classical and contemporary works (including pieces commissioned for the company) in Tucson and in Phoenix, where it performs at the Herberger Theater Center, Symphony Hall, and Gammage Auditorium.

Film

If you're looking for something besides the latest blockbuster, the **Valley Art Theatre** (✉ 509 S. Mill Ave., Tempe, ☎ 602/829–6668) shows major foreign releases and domestic art films.

Galleries

The gallery scene in Phoenix and Scottsdale is so extensive that your best bet is to consult the "art exhibits" listings in the weekly *New Times* or the Friday *Rep Entertainment Guide* put out by the *Arizona Republic*. Or simply stroll down to Main Street and Marshall Way in downtown Scottsdale to view the best art the Valley has to offer.

Theater and Shows

Actors Theatre of Phoenix (✉ Box 1924, Phoenix 85001-1924, ☎ 602/253–6701 or 602/252–8497) is the resident theater troupe at the Herberger. The theater presents a full season of drama, comedy, and musical productions.

Arizona Theatre Company (✉ 808 N. 1st St., ☎ 602/256–6995 or 602/252–8497) is the only resident company in the country with a two-city (Tucson and Phoenix) operation. Productions range from classical dramas to musicals and new works by emerging playwrights. The Phoenix season runs October–May at the Herberger.

Black Theater Troupe (✉ 333 E. Portland St., ☎ 602/258–8128) performs at its own house, the Helen K. Mason Center, a half block from the city's Performing Arts Building on Deck Park. It presents original and contemporary dramas and musical revues, as well as adventurous adaptations.

Childsplay (✉ Box 517, Tempe 85280, ☎ 602/350–8112) is the state's professional theater company for young audiences and families. Rotating through many a venue—Herberger Theater Center, Scottsdale Center for the Arts, and Tempe Performing Arts Center—these players deliver colorful, high-energy performances of works ranging from adaptations of *Charlotte's Web* and *The Velveteen Rabbit* to a theatrical salute to surrealist painter René Magritte and the power of imagination.

Great Arizona Puppet Theatre, temporarily housed in the Town and Country Shopping Center (✉ 20th St. and Camelback Rd., ☎ 602/262–2050), mounts a yearlong cycle of inventive puppet productions that change weekly; it also offers puppetry classes.

Dinner Theaters

Copper State Dinner Theatre (✉ 6727 N. 47th Ave., Glendale, ☎ 602/937–1671), the Valley's oldest troupe, stages light comedy at Max's, a West Valley sports bar, Friday and Saturday nights and Sunday afternoons.

Murder Ink Productions (✉ 1801 S. Jentilly La., Suite C-12, Tempe, ☎ 602/967–6800) presents audience-interactive whodunits at Slim & Curly's Steakhouse (Mesa), Avanti (Scottsdale), Beef Eater's (Phoenix), and Le Rhone's Tropicana Cafe (Phoenix).

Wild West Shows

At **Rawhide Western Town & Steakhouse** (✉ 23023 N. Scottsdale Rd., Scottsdale, ☎ 602/502–1880), the false fronts on the dusty Main Street contain a train depot, saloons, gift shops, and craftspeople. Reenacted Old West shootouts and cheesy souvenirs make this a venue for down home tacky fun. City slickers can take a ride on a stagecoach or gentle burro, and kids will enjoy the Petting Ranch's barn-yard animals. Hayrides travel a short distance into the desert for weekend "Sundown Cookouts" under the stars.

Rockin' R Ranch (⊠ 6136 E. Baseline Rd., Mesa, ☎ 602/832–1539) includes a petting zoo, a reenactment of a wild shoot-out, and—the main attraction—a nightly cookout with a western stage show. Pan for gold or take a wagon ride until the "vittles" are served, followed by music and entertainment. Similar to its competitor, Rawhide, Rockin' R is a better deal as it's all-inclusive.

NIGHTLIFE

Downtown Phoenix, which used to close up at sunset, at last has nightclubs, restaurants, and upscale bars that compete with livelier resorts and clubs in Scottsdale, along Camelback Road in north-central Phoenix, and elsewhere around the Valley.

Among music and dancing styles, country and western has the longest tradition here; jazz, surprisingly, runs a close second. Rock clubs and hotel lounges are also numerous and varied. The Valley attracts a steady stream of pop and rock acts; for concert tickets, try Dillard's (☎ 602/503–5555 or 800/638–4253). Phoenix is getting hipper and more cosmopolitan as it gets older: cigar-lovers or martini-sippers will find a wealth of opportunities to indulge their tastes. There are also over 30 gay and lesbian bars, centered primarily on 7th Avenue, 7th Street, and the stretch of Camelback Road between the two.

The best listings and reviews are in the *New Times* free weekly newspaper, distributed Wednesday, and the *Rep Entertainment Guide* of the *Arizona Republic. PHX Downtown,* a free monthly available in downtown establishments, has an extensive calendar for the neighborhood's events from art exhibits and poetry readings to professional sporting events.

Bars and Lounges

America's Original Sports Bar (⊠ 455 N. 3rd St., Arizona Center, ☎ 602/252–2112) offers more than 40,000 square ft of boisterous fun, with 62 TVs (seven giant screens), indoor basketball, and a sand volleyball court.

AZ88 (✉ 7353 Scottsdale Mall, Scottsdale, ☏ 602/994–5576) has the vibe of a big-city bar and an artful interior. Casual dining and comfortable surroundings make this a perennial favorite of all ages.

Beeloe's Cafe and Underground Bar (✉ 501 S. Mill Ave., Tempe, ☏ 602/894–1230) is everything you'd expect in this hip college town, with eclectic presentations of visual and musical artists. As the name implies, the bar is located in the basement.

Cajun House (✉ 7117 E. 3rd Ave., Scottsdale, ☏ 602/945–5208), currently one of the hottest spots in the area, is the Valley's only Louisiana-themed venue. Join locals who sip Hurricanes while listening to rock, jazz, and Cajun music; on weekends there's a line to get in.

The Famous Door (✉ 7419 Indian Plaza, Scottsdale, ☏ 602/941–4617) specializes in martinis and cigars. Relax to the sounds of local jazz artist Bernie Meisinger on weekends.

Majerle's Sports Grill (✉ 24 N. 2nd St., ☏ 602/253–9004), a new spot opened by former Suns basketball player Dan Majerle, is within striking distance of the major sports facilities and offers a comprehensive menu as well as a bar for post-game celebrations (or sorrow-drowning).

The **Plaza Bar** (✉ 122 N. 2nd St., ☏ 602/252–1234), on the mezzanine of the Hyatt Regency Phoenix, provides a sparkling downtown view. Tables just outside the bar offer a quieter getaway.

Top of the Rock Bar (✉ 2000 W. Westcourt Way, Tempe, ☏ 602/431–2370), the lounge in Top of the Rock restaurant at the Buttes, attracts an older, professional crowd to drink in cocktails and the city's most spectacular view.

Casinos

Just northeast of Scottsdale, **Fort McDowell Casino** (✉ 2 mi east of Shea Blvd. on AZ 87, ☏ 602/843–3678 or 800/843–3678) is popular with the Scottsdale-resort crowd. In addition to the cards, slots, and keno games, offtrack grey-hound wagering takes place in a classy, mahogany room with 18 giant video screens. Take advantage of the casino's Valley-wide shuttle.

Clubs

Bobby McGee's (✉ 7000 E. Shea Blvd., Scottsdale, ☎ 602/998–5591) is the one of the Valley's most popular spots for DJ-spun music.

Downside Risk (✉ 7419 E. Indian Plaza, ☎ 602/945–3304) is a sure bet for a chic, young crowd in the mood to libate and gyrate.

Empire (✉ 4824 N. 24th St., ☎ 602/955–5244) is a happening nightclub, with two full bars, 11 pool tables, and dancing Tuesday–Saturday nights.

Jetz (✉ 7077 E. Camelback Rd., Scottsdale, ☎ 602/970–6001) has three glitzy dance floors, an extensive bar, and a good-looking crowd. The annex, **Stixx,** is filled with billiard tables.

Martini Ranch & MR Sports Bar (✉ 7295 E. Stetson Dr., Scottsdale, ☎ 602/970–0500) attracts singles to its patio where alternative and classic rock bands play every night except Sunday and Tuesday.

Coffeehouses

Willow House (✉ 149 W. McDowell Rd., ☎ 620/252–0272) is a self-described "artist's cove" that draws scores of artsy, bohemian-types—a uniquely fun and funky spot in a city not overflowing with great coffeehouses. Thursday-night poetry readings are a big draw. The espresso flows until midnight on weeknights, 1 AM on weekends.

Comedy

The Improv (✉ 930 E. University Dr., Tempe, ☎ 602/921–9877), part of a national chain, showcases better-known headliners Tuesday–Sunday; shows cost between $10 and $15.

Star Theater (✉ 7117 E. McDowell Rd., Scottsdale, ☎ 602/423–0120) features the "family sensitive" Oxymoron'Z Improvisational Troupe on Friday and Saturday nights and stand-up comics the last two Thursdays of each month; reservations are required.

Country and Western

Handlebar-J (✉ 7116 E. Becker La., Scottsdale, ☎ 602/948–0110) has a lively, 10-gallon-hat–wearing crowd.

At **Mr. Lucky's** (✉ 3660 W. Grand Ave., ☎ 602/246–0686), the granddaddy of Phoenix western clubs, you can dance the two-step all night (or learn it, if you haven't before).

The **Red River Opry** (✉ 730 N. Mill Ave., Tempe, ☎ 602/829–6779) performs foot-stompin' matinee and evening country and bluegrass shows. Reserve your seat in advance.

The Rockin' Horse Saloon (✉ 7316 E. Stetson Dr., Scottsdale, ☎ 602/949–0992) features baby back ribs, live Western music, and dancing in a setting guaranteed to bring out the cowboy or cowgirl in you.

Toolies Country Saloon and Dance Hall (✉ 4231 W. Thomas Rd., ☎ 602/272–3100) has live bands seven nights a week, and often books well-known national acts.

Gay and Lesbian Bars

Ain't Nobody's Business (✉ 3001 E. Indian School Rd., ☎ 602/224–9977) is the most popular lesbian bar in town; you'll also find a few gay men at this "male-friendly" establishment, well-known as one of the most fun in town.

B.S. West (✉ 7125 5th Ave., Scottsdale, ☎ 602/945–9028) draws a yuppie crowd (lots of Campari consumed here) to this location tucked in a shopping center on Scottsdale's main shopping drag.

Charlie's (✉ 727 W. Camelback Rd., ☎ 602/265–0224), a longtime favorite of local gay men, has a country-western look (cowboy hats are the prevailing accessory) and friendly staff.

Crow Bar (⊠ 702 N. Central Ave., ☎ 602/258–8343), is the latest hip spot for young gay men to see and be seen; Phoenicians proclaim it's where the "beautiful people" hang out.

Jazz

For a current schedule of jazz happenings, call the **Jazz in AZ Hotline** (☎ 602/254–4545).

Azz Jazz Cafe (⊠ 1906 E. Camelback Rd., ☎ 602/263–8482) is an intimate spot designed to showcase jazz combos.

J. Chew & Co. (⊠ 7320 Scottsdale Mall, Scottsdale, ☎ 602/946–2733) is a cozy, popular spot with indoor and outdoor seating. It's the place to find up-and-coming jazz performers while enjoying a tasty hot or cold sandwich.

Orbit Cafe (⊠ 40 E. Camelback Rd., ☎ 602/265–2354) has live jazz and blues Thursday–Sunday in a contemporary art-deco setting with a casual ambience.

Timothy's (⊠ 6335 N. 16th St., ☎ 602/277–7634) joins fine French-influenced southwestern cuisine with top jazz performances from 8:30 to 12:30 nightly, and there's no cover charge.

Microbreweries

Bandersnatch Brew Pub (⊠ 125 E. 5th St., Tempe, ☎ 602/966–4438) is a popular, unhurried student hangout that features a large collection of brewed-daily *cervezas*.

Coyote Springs Brewing Co. (⊠ 4883 N. 20th St. at Camelback Rd., ☎ 602/468–0403; ⊠ 122 E. Washington St., ☎ 602/256–6645), the oldest brewpub in Phoenix, has delicious handcrafted ales and lagers, and a thriving patio scene at the 20th Street location. Try a raspberry brew.

Hops! Bistro & Brewery (⊠ 2584 E. Camelback Rd., Biltmore Fashion Park, ☎ 602/468–0500; ⊠ 7000 E. Camelback Rd., Scottsdale Fashion Square, ☎ 602/945–4677; ⊠ 8668 E. Shea Blvd., Scottsdale, ☎ 602/998–7777) serves up bistro cuisine and fills frothy-headed mugs with amber and wheat drafts from the display brewery.

Rock and Blues

Blue Note (✉ 8708 E. McDowell Rd., Scottsdale, ☎ 602/946–6227), unlike its famous namesake in New York City, focuses on blues instead of bebop.

Char's Has the Blues (✉ 4631 N. 7th Ave., ☎ 602/230–0205) is the top Valley blues club with nightly bands.

Long Wong's (✉ 701 S. Mill Ave., Tempe, ☎ 602/966–3147) may not be the most elegant joint you'll ever see, but huge crowds of student types pack the crowded, graffiti-covered room to catch the sounds of down-and-dirty rock and roll.

Mason Jar (✉ 2303 E. Indian School Rd., ☎ 602/956–6271) has a nightly schedule of rock bands.

Rhythm Room (✉ 1019 E. Indian School Rd., ☎ 602/265–4842) hosts a variety of local and touring blues artists.

6 Outdoor Activities and Sports

PARTICIPANT SPORTS

When participating in outdoor activities in the Valley, be aware that the desert heat imposes its particular restraints—even in winter, hikers and cyclists should wear lightweight opaque clothing, a hat or visor, and high UV-rated sunglasses. Carry a water supply of one quart per person for each hour of activity. The intensity of the sun makes strong sunscreen (SPF 15 or higher) a must, and don't forget to apply it to hands and feet. From May 1 to October 1, don't jog or hike from one hour after sunrise until a half hour before sunset. During those times, the air is so hot and dry that your body will lose moisture—and burn calories—at a dangerous, potentially lethal rate. Don't head out to desert areas at night to jog or hike in the summer; that's when rattlesnakes and scorpions are out hunting.

Bicycling

The Valley's terrain is relatively level. Be sure to have a helmet and a mirror when riding in the streets: there are few adequate bike lanes.

Scottsdale's Indian Bend Wash (⊠ Along Hayden Rd., from Shea Blvd. south to Indian School Rd.) has bikeable paths winding among its golf courses and ponds. **Pinnacle Peak,** about 25 mi northeast of downtown Phoenix, is a popular place to take bikes for the ride north to Carefree and Cave Creek, or east and south over the mountain pass and down to the Verde River, toward Fountain Hills. Mountain bikers like **Trail 100,** which runs throughout the Phoenix Mountain preserve (enter at Dreamy Draw park, just east of the intersection of Northern Ave. and 16th St.). **Cave Creek** and **Carefree,** in the foothills about 30 mi northeast of Phoenix, offer a wide range of stopover options. **South Mountain Park** (☞ Hiking, *below*) is the prime site for mountain bikers, with its 40-plus mi of trails—some of them with challenging ascents and all of them quiet and scenic.

To get in touch with fellow bikers and find out about regular and special-event rides and races, contact the **Arizona**

Bicycle Club (Gene or Sylvia Berlatsky, ✉ Box 7191, Phoenix 85011, ☎ 602/264–5478 or 602/279–6674), the state's largest group. Popular Sunday-morning rides start in Phoenix's Granada Park (✉ 20th St. and Maryland Ave.) and end up at a local breakfast spot. **Arizona Scenic Biking** (☎ 602/905–2453) provides hotel pickup, mountain bikes and equipment, and a CPR-certified tour leader for half-day rides. **Desert Biking Adventures** (✉ 7119 E. Shea Blvd., #109–247, Scottsdale 85254, ☎ 602/320–4602 or 888/249–2453) offers two-, three-, and four-hour mountain-biking excursions through the Sonoran desert.

For rentals, contact **Wheels N' Gear** (✉ 7607 E. McDowell Rd., Scottsdale, ☎ 602/945–2881). For detailed maps of bike paths, contact **Phoenix Parks and Recreation** (☎ 602/262–6861). If you want to bring your own bike, most airlines accommodate bikes as luggage, provided they are dismantled and put into a box. Call to see if your airline sells bike boxes (about $5; bike bags are at least $100) although they are often free at bike shops. International travelers can sometimes substitute a bike for a piece of checked luggage for free; otherwise, it will cost about $100. Domestic and Canadian airlines charge a $25–$50 fee.

Four-Wheeling

Take a Jeep through the backcountry to experience the desert terrain's saguaro-covered mountains and curious rock formations. A number of companies offer four-wheeling packages for $50–$75 for short excursions.

Arizona Awareness Desert Jeep Tours (✉ 835 E. Brown St., ☎ 602/947–7852) ventures down to the Verde River on its own trail and offers wilderness cookouts.

Arrowhead Desert Jeep Tours (☎ 602/942–3361 or 800/514–9063), run by a self-described "hard core prospector that fell in love with tourism," offers adventures that include gold panning on a private claim, cookouts, cattle drives, river crossings, and Native American dancers.

Carefree Jeep Adventures (☎ 602/488–0023 or 800/294–5337) travels into the Tonto National Forest on rugged old stage and mining roads, stopping for botany lessons, explorations of Hohokam ruins and a gold mine, and a six-gun target shoot along the way.

Scottsdale Jeep Rentals (☎ 602/951–2191) rents Jeeps and provides free trail maps to those who prefer to drive themselves and eschew the company of a talkative guide.

Golf

Arizona has more golf courses per capita than any other state west of the Mississippi River, an embarrassment of riches that, coupled with its surfeit of sunny days, makes the Grand Canyon State a golfer's paradise. The world-class courses are among Arizona's major industries, with new spots popping up seemingly on a daily basis: more than 100 courses are available (some lighted at night), and the PGA's Southwest section has its headquarters here. For a detailed listing, contact the **Arizona Golf Association** (⊠ 7226 N. 16th St., Phoenix 85020, ☎ 602/944–3035 or 800/458–8484).

Ahwatukee Country Club (⊠ 12432 S. 48th St., Phoenix, ☎ 602/893–9772), an upscale course just south of South Mountain Park, is semiprivate but also has a public driving range.

Arizona Biltmore (⊠ 24th St. and Missouri Ave., Phoenix, ☎ 602/955–9655), the granddaddy of Phoenix golf courses, offers two 18-hole PGA championship courses, lessons, and clinics.

Encanto Park (⊠ 2775 N. 15th Ave., Phoenix, ☎ 602/253–3963) is an attractive, affordable public course.

Gold Canyon Golf Club (⊠ 6100 S. Kings Ranch Rd., Gold Canyon, ☎ 602/982–9090) is a desert course with a stunning Superstition Mountains backdrop.

Grayhawk Golf Club (⊠ 19600 N. Pima Rd., Scottsdale, ☎ 602/502–1800), a high-end daily-user course, has championship design by Tom Fazio and mint conditioning.

Hillcrest Golf Club (⊠ 20002 N. Star Ridge, Sun City West, ☎ 602/584–1500) is the best course in the Sun Cities, with 179 acres of well-designed turf.

Papago Golf Course (⊠ 5595 E. Moreland St., Phoenix, ☎ 602/275–8428) is a low-price public course in a scenic city setting. Tee times can be hard to come by here at Phoenix's best municipal course.

Raven Golf Club at South Mountain (⊠ 3636 E. Baseline Rd., Phoenix, ☎ 602/437–3800) has thousands of drought-resistant Aleppo pines and Lombardy poplars, making it a cool, shady haven for summertime golfers.

Sun Ridge Canyon (⊠ 13100 N. Sun Ridge Dr., Fountain Hills, ☎ 602/837–5100) is an 18-hole championship course with an inspiring view of the canyon scenery.

Thunderbird Country Club (⊠ 701 E. Thunderbird Trail, Phoenix, ☎ 602/243–1262) has 18 holes of championship-rated play on the north slopes of South Mountain. Sweeping views of the city are a bonus.

Tournament Players Club of Scottsdale (⊠ 17020 N. Hayden Rd., Scottsdale, ☎ 602/585–3600), a 36-hole course created by Tom Weiskopf and Jay Morrish, is the site of the PGA Phoenix Open.

Troon North (⊠ 10320 E. Dynamite Blvd., Scottsdale, ☎ 602/585–5300) offers a challenging 36-hole course, designed by Weiskopf and Morrish, that makes excellent use of the existing desert.

Health Clubs

The **Arizona Athletic Club** (⊠ 1425 W. 14th St., Tempe, ☎ 602/894–2281), near the airport at the border between Tempe and Scottsdale, is the Valley's largest facility. Non-members pay a day rate of $12, but the club has arrangements with some area hotels.

Jazzercise (☎ 602/893–1557 or 800/348–4748) has 27 franchised sites in the Valley.

Naturally Women (⊠ 2827 W. Peoria Ave., Phoenix, ☎ 602/678–4000; ⊠ 3320 S. Price Rd., Tempe, ☎ 602/838–8800; ⊠ 7750 E. McDowell Rd., Phoenix, ☎ 602/947–8300), closed Sunday, focuses on women's needs, from health profiles to diet and exercise programs; it offers one free visit, then a day rate of $10 thereafter.

The **YMCA** (☎ 602/528–5540) offers full facilities—including weight rooms, aerobics classes, pool, and racquetball privileges—to nonmembers at several Valley locations. Rates are $8 per day.

Hiking

The Valley has some of the best desert mountain hiking and most heavily used trails in the world—the **Phoenix Mountain Preserve System** (☎ 602/495–0022), in the mountains that surround the city, has its own park rangers who can help plan your hikes. The **Sierra Club** (☎ 602/253–8633) leads a variety of wilderness treks in the area.

Camelback Mountain (✉ North of Camelback Rd. on 48th St., ☎ 602/256–3220), another landmark hike, has no park, and the trails are challenging. This is for intermediate to experienced hikers.

The **Papago Peaks** (✉ Van Buren St. and Galvin Pkwy., ☎ 602/256–3110) were sacred sites for the Tohono O'odham tribe and probably the Hohokam before them. The soft sandstone peaks contain accessible caves, some petroglyphs, and splendid views of much of the Valley. This is a good spot for family hikes.

Squaw Peak Summit Trail (✉ 2701 E. Squaw Peak Dr., just north of Lincoln Dr., ☎ 602/262–7901) ascends the landmark mountain at a steep 19% grade, but children can handle the 1.2-mi hike if adults take it slowly—allow about 1½ hours for each direction. Plenty of locals risk twisted ankles to jog this peak after work. Call ahead to schedule an easy hike with a ranger who introduces desert geology, flora, and fauna.

South Mountain Park (✉ 10919 S. Central Ave., ☎ 602/495–0222) is the jewel of the city's Mountain Park Preserves. Its mountains and arroyos contain more than 40 mi of marked and maintained trails—all open to hikers, horseback riders, and mountain bikers. It also has three autoaccessible lookout points, with 65-mi sight lines. Rangers can help you plan hikes to some of the 200 petroglyph sites.

Horseback Riding

More than two dozen stables and equestrian tour outfitters in the Valley attest to the saddle's enduring importance in Arizona—even in this auto-dominated metropolis.

All Western Stables (✉ 10220 S. Central Ave., Phoenix, ☏ 602/276–5862), one of several stables at the entrance to South Mountain Park, offers rentals, guided rides, hayrides, and group cookouts.

MacDonald's Ranch (✉ 26540 N. Scottsdale Rd., Scottsdale, ☏ 602/585–0239) offers one- and two-hour trail rides, as well as guided breakfast, lunch, and dinner rides through desert foothills above Scottsdale.

Superstition Stables (✉ Windsong and Meridian Rds., Apache Junction, ☏ 602/982–6353) is licensed to lead tours throughout the entire Superstition Mountains area for more experienced riders; easier rides are also available.

Hot-Air Ballooning

A sunrise or sunset hot-air-balloon ascent is a remarkable desert sightseeing experience. The average fee—there are more than three dozen companies to chose from—is $135 per person and hotel pickup is usually included. Since flight paths and landing sites vary with wind speeds and directions, a roving land crew follows each balloon in flight. Time in the air is generally between 1 and 1½ hours, but allow three hours for the total excursion. Be prepared for changing temperatures as the sun rises or sets, but it's not actually any colder up in the balloon.

Adventures Out West (☏ 602/996–6100 or 800/755–0935) will send you home with a free video of your flight taped from the balloon.

Hot Air Expeditions (☏ 602/502–6999 or 800/831–7610) offers the best ballooning in Phoenix. Flights are long, the staff is charming, and the gourmet treats are out of this world.

Unicorn Balloon Company (☏ 602/991–3666 or 800/468–2478), operating since 1978, is run by the state's ballooning examiner for the FAA. At Scottsdale Airport, it offers free pickup at many area hotels.

Jogging

Phoenix's unique 200-mi network of canals provides a naturally cooled scenic track throughout the metro area. Two other popular jogging areas are Phoenix's **Encanto Park,** 3 mi northwest of Civic Plaza, and Scottsdale's **Indian Bend Wash,** which runs for more than 5 mi along Hayden Road. Both have lagoons and tree-shaded greens.

Rockhounding

The Department of Mines and Mineral Resources (✉ 1502 W. Washington St., Phoenix 85007, ☎ 602/255−3795) is an excellent source of information about specimens that can be found in the area.

Sailplaning

At the Estrella Sailport, **Arizona Soaring Inc.** (✉ Box 858, Maricopa 85239, ☎ 602/821−2903 or 800/861−2318) gives sailplane rides in a basic trainer or high-performance plane for prices ranging from $60 to $80. A wild 15-minute acrobatic flight is $95.

Tennis

Many hotels either have their own courts are are affiliated with a private or municipal facility.

Gardiner's Resort on Camelback (✉ 5700 E. McDonald Dr., Scottsdale 85253, ☎ 602/948−2100 or 800/245−2051) is one of the country's best tennis-oriented resorts.

Hole-in-the-Wall Racquet Club (✉ 7677 N. 16th St., Pointe Hilton at Squaw Peak Resort, ☎ 602/997−2626) has eight paved courts available for same-day reservation at $15 per hour.

Kiwanis Park Recreation Center (✉ 6111 S. All America Way, Tempe, ☎ 602/350−5201, ext. 4) has 15 lighted premier-surface courts (all for same-day or one-day-advance reserve). Before 5 PM, courts rent for $4.50, after 5 PM, the rate is $6; $2 drop-in programs are offered for single players weekdays, 10:30−noon.

Mountain View Tennis Center (⊠ 1104 E. Grovers Ave., Phoenix, ☎ 602/788–6088), just north of Bell Road, is a Phoenix city facility with 20 lighted courts that can be reserved for $3 for 90 minutes of singles play during the day; after dark, the light fee is $2.20.

Phoenix Civic Plaza Sports Complex (⊠ 121 E. Adams St., Phoenix, ☎ 602/256–4120) has three lighted rooftop courts available for $4–$6.

Phoenix Tennis Center (⊠ 6330 N. 21st Ave., Phoenix, ☎ 602/249–3712), a city facility with 22 lighted hard courts, charges $1.50 per person for 1½ hours on the courts; if it's after dark, add a $2.20 light fee.

Watering Hole Racquet Club (⊠ 901–C E. Saguaro Dr., Phoenix, ☎ 602/997–7237) has nine hard, lighted courts that rent for $15 per hour.

Tubing

In a region not known for water, tubing—riding an inner tube down calm water and mild rapids—has become very popular on the Salt and Verde rivers. Outfitters include **Salt River Recreation** (⊠ Usery Pass and Power Rds., Mesa, ☎ 602/984–3305), conveniently located and offering shuttle-bus service to and from your starting point. Tubes are $8 per day, all day 9–4; tubing season runs May–September.

SPECTATOR SPORTS

Auto Racing

Phoenix International Raceway (⊠ 7602 S. 115th Ave., Avondale, ☎ 602/252–3833), the Valley's NASCAR track, hosts the Skoal Bandit Copper World Classic, Phoenix 200 Indy Car race, and Phoenix 500 NASCAR race.

Balloon Racing

The **Thunderbird Hot-Air-Balloon Classic** (☎ 602/978–7208) has grown into a schedule of festivities surrounding the national invitational balloon race, held the first weekend in November. You haven't lived till you've seen the Valley skies filled with almost 100 brightly colored balloons.

Baseball

The **Arizona Diamondbacks** (⊠ Box 2095, Phoenix, 85001, ☏ 602/514–8400), Phoenix's Major League baseball team, made its debut in the 1998 season. Games are held next to the America West Arena at the brand-new **Bank One Ballpark** (⊠ 401 E. Jefferson St., ☏ 602/462–6000), a unique 48,500-seat stadium with a retractable roof and a natural grass playing surface. With 79 luxury boxes, six private party suites, and a slew of restaurants, the stadium is a welcome addition to the downtown entertainment scene.

During spring training in March, the **Oakland Athletics** are at Phoenix Municipal Stadium (☏ 602/392–0074), the **San Francisco Giants** are at Scottsdale Stadium (☏ 602/990–7972 or 415/467–8000 off-season), the **Anaheim Angels** are at Diablo Stadium in Tempe (☏ 602/350–5205 or 888/99–halos off-season), and the **Milwaukee Brewers** are at the Compadre Stadium in Chandler (☏ 602/895–1200). Both the **San Diego Padres** and the **Seattle Mariners** train at Preoria Stadium (☏ 602/878–4337), 30 minutes from downtown Phoenix.

Cactus League games start at the end of February; **Dillard's** (☏ 602/503–5555) sells tickets.

Basketball

The **Phoenix Suns** (⊠ 201 E. Jefferson St., ☏ 602/379–7867 or 602/379–7900) continue to fill all 19,000 spectator seats in the America West Arena; Valley basketball fans are fiercely loyal to the team. Tip-off is usually at 7 PM.

Football

The **Arizona Cardinals** (⊠ Box 888, Phoenix, ☏ 888/386–8497 for schedule and tickets), is the area's professional football team, which plays at ASU's Sun Devil Stadium on Stadium Drive in Tempe.

Also held at Sun Devil Stadium, the **Fiesta Bowl** (☎ 602/350–0911) is one of college football's most important bowl games. It's held on New Year's Eve.

The **Arizona Rattlers** (☎ 602/514–8383) are part of the summer AFL (Arena Football League) and play at the America West Arena. The national league is in its 12th season and runs from April through August. Arena football is an offensive, high-scoring game with a 50-yard field, rebound nets in the end-zones, and a dasherboard perimeter. Players stay after the game to meet with fans.

Golf

The **Phoenix Open** (☎ 602/585–4334), played in January at the Tournament Players Club of Scottsdale, is a major PGA Tour event drawing an estimated 400,000 spectators each year. In March, women compete in the **Standard Register PING Tournament** (☎ 602/942–0000), at the Moon Valley Country Club.

Hockey

The **Phoenix Coyotes** (☎ 602/379–7825) face off in the America West Arena; whether you come for the cross-checking, hooking, or to watch the Zamboni, you'll revel in the extravagance that is artificial ice in the desert.

Rodeos

The **Parada del Sol,** held each January by the Scottsdale Jaycees (✉ Box 292, Scottsdale 85251, ☎ 602/990–3179), includes a rodeo, a lavish parade famed for its silver-studded saddle, and a 200-mi daredevil ride from Holbrook down the Mogollon Rim to Scottsdale by the Hashknife Pony Express. The **Rodeo of Rodeos,** sponsored in March by the Phoenix Jaycees (✉ 4133 N. 7th St., ☎ 602/263–8671), has one of the Southwest's oldest and best parades. The **World's Oldest Rodeo** (✉ Box 2037, Prescott 86302, ☎ 800/358–1888), held each July as part of Frontier Days, gives the Phoenix rodeos a run for their money.

7 Shopping

SINCE ITS RESORTS BEGAN multiplying in the 1930s and 1940s, Phoenix has acquired a healthy share of high-style clothiers and leisure-wear boutiques. But well before that, western clothes were dominant here—jeans and boots, cotton shirts and dresses, 10-gallon hats and bola ties (the state's official neckwear). They still are.

In the past decade, Sun Belt awareness has brought a tide of interest in southwestern furnishing styles as well, from the pastels of the desert mountains and skies to handmade lodgepole furniture of the pueblo and rancho. These—as well as Mexican tiles and tinware, wrought iron and copper work, courtyard fountains and paper flowers—have never died out here. Always an essential part of the way southwesterners shape their homes, work spaces, and public places, these crafts have flourished in the current revival.

On the scene long before, of course, were the arts of the Southwest's true natives—Navajo weavers, sand painters, and silversmiths; Hopi weavers and kachina-doll carvers; Pima and Tohono O'odham (Papago) basket makers and potters; and many more. Inspired by the region's rich cultural traditions, contemporary artists have flourished here as well, making Phoenix—and in particular Scottsdale, a city with more art galleries than gas stations—one of the Southwest's largest art centers (alongside Santa Fe, New Mexico).

Most of the Valley's power shopping is concentrated in central Phoenix and downtown Scottsdale. But auctions and antiques shops cluster in odd places—and as treasure hunters know, you've always got to have an eye open.

Antiques and Collectibles

Downtown Glendale along Glendale Avenue and the side streets between 57th and 59th avenues has dozens of antiques stores and a "Gaslight Antique Walk" on the third Thursday evening of each month (every Thursday in December).

Glendale Square Antiques (⊠ 7009 N. 58th Ave., ☎ 602/ 435–9952) has a nice collection of glassware, china, and vintage watches. **House of Gera** (⊠ 7025 N. 58th Ave., ☎ 842–4631) specializes in Victoriana, particularly jewelry, and houses the offbeat Rosato Nursing Museum. **The Mad Hatter** (⊠ 5734 W. Glendale Ave., ☎ 602/931–1991) is a cavernous space with everything from crystal and Fiestaware to old metal wheels and dusty saddles.

Scottsdale Antique Destination is a grouping of four stores: **Antique Centre** (⊠ 2012 N. Scottsdale Rd., ☎ 602/675–9500), **Antique Trove** (⊠ 2020 N. Scottsdale Rd., ☎ 602/9497–6074), and **Antiques Super-Mall** (⊠ 1900 N. Scottsdale Rd., ☎ 602/874–2900) all have fine antiques and offbeat collectibles, and **Razmataz** (⊠ 2012 N. Scottsdale Rd., ☎ 602/946–9748) offers imported antique and new furniture and decorative items, primarily from Mexico.

Arts and Crafts

Art One (⊠ 4120 N. Marshall Way, Scottsdale, ☎ 602/946–5076) features works by art students of the area; much of what is found here is quite interesting. Invest in an inexpensive painting or sculpture created by a star of tomorrow.

Suzanne Brown Galleries (⊠ 7160 Main St., Scottsdale, ☎ 602/945-8475) has a fabulous collection of innovative glasswork, painting, and other fine arts.

Cosanti Originals (⊠ 6433 Doubletree Ranch Rd., Scottsdale, ☎ 602/948–6145) is the studio where architect Paolo Soleri's famous bronze and ceramic wind chimes are made and sold. You can watch the craftspeople hard at work, then pick out your own (they're surprisingly reasonable).

The **Heard Museum Shop** (⊠ 22 E. Monte Vista Rd., ☎ 602/252–8344) is hands-down the best place in town for southwestern Native American arts and crafts, both traditional and modern. Prices tend to be high but quality is assured, with many one-of-a-kind items among their collection of rugs, kachina dolls, pottery, and other crafts; there's also a wide selection of lower-priced gifts. The back room gallery has the latest in Native painting and lithographs.

Karibu Africa (⊠ 7044 E. 5th Ave., Scottsdale, ☎ 602/874–2599) is the only shop on Fifth Avenue featuring African art, including masks, modern sculpture and jewelry, and such curiosities as a necklace made from an Ethiopian neck scratcher.

LeKAE Galleries (✉ 7175 E. Main St., Scottsdale, ☎ 602/874–2624) is a low-pressure, pleasant place to admire some of today's most exciting work. The friendly and discerning staff has scoured the Southwest and beyond for the best in contemporary painting and sculpture.

Mind's Eye (✉ 4200 N. Marshall Way, Scottsdale, ☎ 602/941–8349) offers an eclectic selection of whimsical art furniture, quilted baskets, bright pottery, and beautifully offbeat kaleidoscopes fashioned from Italian glass, German jewels, and other bits and pieces.

Two Gray Hills (✉ 7142 E. 5th Ave., Scottsdale, ☎ 602/947–1997 or 800/238–0798) deals in Native jewelry, crafts, and kachina dolls. The knowledgeable staff—it's one of the few shops around to regularly employ Native Americans—will walk you through the styles and lore of traditional jewelry. They pledge to beat the price of any neighborhood competitor.

Markets

Guadalupe Farmer's Market (✉ 9210 S. Av. del Yaqui, Guadalupe, ☎ 602/730–1945) has all the fresh ingredients you'd find in a rural Mexican market—tomatillos, varieties of chili peppers (fresh and dried), fresh-ground *masa* (cornmeal) for tortillas, cumin and cilantro, and on and on.

Mercado Mexico (✉ 8212 S. Av. del Yaqui, Guadalupe, ☎ 602/831–5925) carries ceramic, paper, tin, and lacquerware, all at unbeatable prices.

Patriot's Square Marketplace (✉ Patriot's Square Park, Washington St. and Central Ave., ☎ 602/848–1234) sells arts and crafts, locally grown produce, baked goods, and homemade jams and salsas, livening up downtown every Wednesday from 10 AM to 2 PM, October–April.

Shopping Centers

Arizona Mills (✉ 1500 W. Baseline Rd., Tempe, ☎ 602/491–9700), the latest entry in the discount shopping sweepstakes, is a mammoth center featuring almost 200 outlet stores, a food court, cinemas, and faux rain forest.

Biltmore Fashion Park (✉ 24th St. and Camelback Rd., Phoenix, ☎ 602/955–8400) has posh shops lining its open-air walkways, as well as some of the city's most popular restaurants and cafés. **Macy's** and **Saks Fifth Avenue** are its anchors, and high-end designer boutiques are its stock-in-trade—**Via Veneto, Gucci,** and **Polo by Ralph Lauren** are among them. **Cornelia Park** offers an awe-inspiring collection of MacKenzie-Childs, Ltd., glassware as well as furnishings, tiles, and linens. Home to RoxSand, Sam's Cafe, and Wolf-gang Puck's new ObaChine, this center has more fine eating in a small radius than anywhere else in Arizona (☞ Chapter 3).

The Borgata (✉ 6166 N. Scottsdale Rd., ☎ 602/998–1822), a re-creation of the Italian village of San Gimigniano, is one of the Valley's most fashionable places to shop and home to some of Scottsdale's most popular restaurants, including Cafe Terra Cotta (☞ Chapter 3). Shops include **Capriccio** for women's wear, **Stefan Mann** for leather goods, **DaVinci** for menswear, and scores of others. Check out the affordable and intriguing **Mineral & Fossil Gallery** near the Coffee Plantation.

Two-tiered **El Pedregal Festival Marketplace** (✉ Scottsdale Rd. and Carefree Hwy., ☎ 602/488–1072), 30 minutes north of downtown Scottsdale, is an attractive shopping plaza. At the foot of a 250-ft boulder formation, it contains posh boutiques and the **Heard Museum North** (☎ 602/488–9817), a satellite of the downtown Heard with its own gift shop. Visit **Casualis** for men's sportswear, **Carefree Casuals** for "wearable" art for women, **Conrad** for custom leather goods, and **Canyon Lifestyles** for Southwestern furniture and decor items. In the spring and summer there are Thursday-night concerts in the courtyard amphitheater.

Metrocenter (✉ I–17 and Peoria Ave., ☎ 602/997–2641), on the west side of Phoenix, is the kind of enclosed double-deck, Muzak-choked sterile environment that made "mall" a four-letter word. Anchor department stores are **Dillard's, JCPenney, Macy's, Robinsons-May,** and **Sears.** Adjacent to the mall, a roller coaster zips through Taj-Mahal–

esque minarets at **Castles 'N' Coasters** (⊠ 9445 N. Metro Pkwy. E, ☎ 602/997–7575), where a miniature-golf park and video-game palace round out the fun.

Mill Avenue in Tempe is the main drag for ASU's student population; small, interesting shops and eateries make for great browsing or just hanging out. **Urban Outfitters** (⊠ 545 S. Mill Ave., ☎ 602/966–7250) sells rough-edged, trendy gear and affordable housewares. The way-cool **Changing Hands Bookstore** (⊠ 414 Mill Ave., ☎ 602/966–0203) has three stories of new and used books and an inviting atmosphere that will tempt you to linger—as many students do.

Paradise Valley Mall (⊠ Cactus Rd. and Tatum Blvd., ☎ 602/996–8840), in northeastern Phoenix, is an older mall, anchored by Macy's department store.

At boisterous **Scottsdale Fashion Square** (⊠ Scottsdale and Camelback Rds., Scottsdale, ☎ 602/941–2140), retractable skylights open to reveal sunny skies above. Besides having Robinsons-May and Dillard's, it is anchored by **Neiman Marcus** (check out the hanging Paolo Soleri sculpture above the Neiman's elevator). The collection of stores runs toward the pricey chains including **J. Crew, Jessica McClintock,** and **Artafax. FAO Schwarz,** the **Disney Store,** and **Warner Bros. Studio Store** are attractions for kids.

Superstition Springs Center (⊠ AZ 60 and Superstition Springs Rd., Mesa, ☎ 602/832–0212), 30 mi east of Phoenix, has the usual complement of shops and eateries, plus a pleasant outdoor cactus garden to stroll in. The handsome indoor carousel and 15-ft Gila-monster slide keep the kids occupied.

INDEX

✕ = restaurant, 🏨 = hotel

WHEREVER YOU TRAVEL, *H*ELP IS NEVER FAR AWAY.

From planning your trip to providing travel assistance along the way, American Express® Travel Service Offices are always there to help you do more.

Phoenix

American Express Travel Service
2508 East Camelback Road
Biltmore Fashion Park
602/468-1199

Bon Voyage Travel, Inc.
400 North Fifth Street
Suite 100
602/257-8878

do more AMERICAN EXPRESS®

Travel
www.americanexpress.com/travel

American Express Travel Service Offices
are located throughout the United States.
For the office nearest you, call 1-800-AXP-3429.